New Directions for
Higher Education

Betsy O. Barefoot
Jillian L. Kinzie
Co-editors

# Reclaiming Higher Education's Purpose in Leadership Development

Kathy L. Guthrie
Laura Osteen
Editors

Number 174 • Summer 2016
Jossey-Bass
San Francisco

RECLAIMING HIGHER EDUCATION'S PURPOSE IN LEADERSHIP DEVELOPMENT
*Kathy L. Guthrie, Laura Osteen*
New Directions for Higher Education, no. 174
*Betsy O. Barefoot and Jillian L. Kinzie*, Co-editors

Microfilm copies of issues and articles are available in 16mm and 35mm, as well as microfiche in 105mm, through University Microfilms Inc., 300 North Zeeb Road, Ann Arbor, MI 48106-1346.

NEW DIRECTIONS FOR HIGHER EDUCATION (ISSN 0271-0560, electronic ISSN 1536-0741) is part of The Jossey-Bass Higher and Adult Education Series and is published quarterly by Wiley Subscription Services, Inc., A Wiley Company, at Jossey-Bass, One Montgomery Street, Suite 1200, San Francisco, CA 94104-4594. POSTMASTER: Send address changes to New Directions for Higher Education, Jossey-Bass, One Montgomery Street, Suite 1200, San Francisco, CA 94104-4594.

*New Directions for Higher Education* is indexed in Current Index to Journals in Education (ERIC); Higher Education Abstracts.

Individual subscription rate (in USD): $89 per year US/Can/Mex, $113 rest of world; institutional subscription rate: $335 US, $375 Can/Mex, $409 rest of world. Single copy rate: $29. Electronic only–all regions: $89 individual, $335 institutional; Print & Electronic–US: $98 individual, $402 institutional; Print & Electronic–Canada/Mexico: $98 individual, $442 institutional; Print & Electronic–Rest of World: $122 individual, $476 institutional.

Editorial correspondence should be sent to the Co-editor, Betsy O. Barefoot, Gardner Institute, Box 72, Brevard, NC 28712.

Cover design: Wiley
Cover Images: © Lava 4 images | Shutterstock

www.josseybass.com

# CONTENTS

# EDITORS' NOTES

The goal of educating students who are prepared to lead has been a hallmark of higher education in the United States since Harvard College opened its doors in 1636. While some characteristics of higher education have remained constant, the context of the college experience and the concepts of leader and leadership have drastically changed over the past centuries. Who is going to college, how colleges and courses are designed, what degrees and activities students engage in, and the enduring question of why higher education exists are dynamic questions impacting the structure, resources, environment, and outcomes of higher education in the United States. Along with these contextual changes, the understanding, study, and teaching of leaders and leadership have evolved. Moving from the model of White, privileged men who were born to lead, educators have arrived at postindustrial models of leadership and now recognize that leaders are made. With this realization, campus-based programs of leadership learning are growing on college campuses across the globe. At their best, these programs create intentional, theory-based, leadership-learning experiences that increase the diversity, distribution, and availability of leadership education to all students. Campus-based leadership development programs also serve as beacons to highlight our shared expectations for college graduates to make positive change in their local and global communities and chosen professions. While we celebrate the existence and growth of leadership centers across student and academic affairs departments, the decentralization of leadership programs on many campuses has led to content silos and the loss of integrated, collaborative efforts.

In order to develop the quality and quantity of diverse leaders necessary to create the change our global society is calling for, institutions must reclaim leadership development as a central purpose of higher education and embrace leadership development across disciplines, thereby making it everyone's business. This volume focuses on our collective and unique capacity as higher education faculty, staff, and stakeholders to leverage and align resources with leadership learning across college and university departments and initiatives. It also seeks to educate all of us on the purposes and processes of weaving leadership development into the fabric of higher education.

NEW DIRECTIONS FOR HIGHER EDUCATION, no. 174, Summer 2016   © 2016 Wiley Periodicals, Inc.
Published online in Wiley Online Library (wileyonlinelibrary.com)  •  DOI: 10.1002/he.20184

It is critical that readers and interpreters of this volume's ideas understand how the editors and chapter authors conceptualize *leader* and *leadership*. The authors in this publication ascribe to a postindustrial leadership paradigm (Rost, 1993) that distinguishes the complexity of engaging in a leadership process from simply holding a position of power to a process of intending real change. Although specific chapters may rely on unique definitions, they are all written from a perspective of leadership as a capacity to work collaboratively with others to create change, solve adaptive challenges, and/or create contexts for group and/or organizational evolution. Leaders are the individuals engaged in this behavior, and if students choose to do so, they can learn, engage, and become leaders. This paradigm challenges the ever-present and ill-advised belief that only those with formal authority can solve the most pressing problems our local, state, national, and global communities are facing. Our students are not only becoming future leaders, but they are also leaders now in their very real worlds, collaboratively solving complex problems and engaging together to address social ills.

The development of students' identities and capacities to lead in their professional, personal, and communal lives has been and currently remains a higher education imperative and is the responsibility of all who work toward the betterment of our students. In this volume, we explore leadership education for undergraduate students from an institutional perspective. We will provide a foundation for faculty, administrators, policymakers, and student affairs professionals to understand the need for and to assist in the development of leadership-learning programs across disciplines, pedagogies, and departments. This volume explores *why* we should focus on reclaiming the purpose of higher education and embrace leadership development across disciplines; it then moves on to *how* we can do this and *what* this may look like. Finally, we end with *how* we know leadership development across disciplines actually happened.

In Chapter 1, Vivechkanand "V" Chunoo and Laura Osteen address the *why*—why we should reclaim the purpose of higher education as a primary environment for the development of future leaders. Chapter 1 connects the purpose, context, and mission of higher education and its direct alignment with the calling, environment, and resources to provide leadership education.

Chapters 2 through 5 then look at the *how* by examining four pedagogical and practical tools for integrating leadership learning across the curriculum. In Chapter 2, Kathy L. Guthrie and Kathleen Callahan discuss how leadership education aligns with liberal studies and specific competencies that enhance each approach. In Chapter 3, Sara E. Thompson and Richard A. Couto discuss problem-based learning and how this pedagogy can strengthen future leaders' abilities to lead. Vijay Pendakur and Sara C. Furr in Chapter 4 explore through personal narratives how institutions can create spaces for such conversations to occur while developing future leaders. In Chapter 5, Daniel M. Jenkins and Anthony C. Andenoro focus on how leadership education offers a distinctive opportunity to improve critical thinking.

Moving from *how* to *what*, Chapters 6 and 7 explore the content of leader and leadership education. With a focus on the specific knowledge, skills, and values leadership education provides across disciplines, T. W. Cauthen III explores the relationship between educational involvement and academic autonomy in Chapter 6, and Scott J. Allen, Marcy Levy Shankman, and Paige Haber-Curran discuss the emotionally intelligent leadership model in Chapter 7. The emotional intelligent leadership model looks at consciousness of context, consciousness of self, and consciousness of others and explores the 21 capacities that define the emotionally intelligent leader.

Finally, in Chapter 8, Corey Seemiller discusses *how* we know the outcomes of leadership education and the importance of leadership competency development for all of higher education. This chapter is based on data from academic accrediting organizations and expands on how using competency-based models creates strong leadership education programs.

We hope you enjoy the ideas and reflections of these leadership educators; moreover, our hope is that these thoughts are relevant to your work in developing all students' leadership capacities across the curriculum. The diversity of thought and ideas reflected here is a testament to the dynamic work occurring in the field of leadership studies. We are appreciative of Antron Mahoney and Chris Ruiz de Esparza's reflective and thoughtful edits to enhance the connectedness of this volume.

For all of us, leadership learning is a lifelong endeavor; we look forward to learning from your reactions and experiences as together we enhance and develop collegiate leadership programs across disciplines. Let us together move forward in reclaiming higher education's purpose and practice of developing the leaders and problem solvers of this generation and the next.

Kathy L. Guthrie
Laura Osteen
Editors

## Reference

Rost, J. C. (1993). *Leadership for the twenty-first century*. Westport, CT: Praeger.

*KATHY L. GUTHRIE is an associate professor in the higher education program at Florida State University. She serves as the coordinator of the Undergraduate Certificate in Leadership Studies and teaches courses in leadership development.*

*LAURA OSTEEN is the director of the Center for Leadership and Social Change at Florida State University. The center transforms lives through leadership education, identity development, and community engagement.*

NEW DIRECTIONS FOR HIGHER EDUCATION • DOI: 10.1002/he

**1**

*This chapter calls on higher education to reclaim its role in leadership education. Specifically it examines higher education's purpose, context, and mission as clarion calls to embed leadership education throughout higher education institutions and focuses on why this is important.*

# Purpose, Mission, and Context: The Call for Educating Future Leaders

*Vivechkanand Chunoo, Laura Osteen*

This volume is grounded in the belief that institutions of higher education must reclaim their unique role in developing the leadership capacity of our nation. We argue that the purpose, mission, and context of higher education should directly align with the calling, environment, and resources necessary to provide leadership education. Beyond alignment, this chapter makes the case that across the diverse range of universities and colleges, the development of students' capacities to lead in their professional, personal, and communal lives is a higher education imperative. Ultimately, we assert that leadership education is the responsibility of all who work toward the betterment of undergraduates, and only through collaboration can the call for leadership education be answered.

Through discussing the purposes of higher education, mission-based structures, and contexts of diverse institutions, this chapter outlines the motivation of leadership educators and the rationale for the work they do across higher education settings. This work is not limited to a specific type of institution, academic discipline, or department. As described in several chapters of this volume, leadership learning is a collaborative, interdisciplinary, and campus-wide endeavor that involves a wide range of students, faculty, staff, and community partners. It is an institutional commitment. Leadership learning involves education, training, development, and engagement; its impact on students influences our political, economic, communal, and educational realities. Across local and global communities, the leadership capacity of citizens of all ages determines our collective future. Therefore, while leadership education is everyone's business, the purpose,

NEW DIRECTIONS FOR HIGHER EDUCATION, no. 174, Summer 2016 © 2016 Wiley Periodicals, Inc.
Published online in Wiley Online Library (wileyonlinelibrary.com) • DOI: 10.1002/he.20185

mission, and context-based work of higher education call for its unique and specific role in the teaching and learning of leadership.

## Purposes of Higher Education

From sustaining a democracy to gaining a liberal education or building a skilled workforce, the purposes of higher education are, and historically have been, subjects of significant debate. The philosophical struggle for the heart of higher education in the United States lies in the following question: Is the purpose of college to ensure a good job after graduation, to provide a broad and deep humanities education, or to create an engaged citizenry (Tugend, 2012)? Despite the rich, three-century history of American higher education, there continues to be widespread disagreement over its fundamental purposes. It stands to reason, however, that its influence on contemporary society is undeniable.

Historians, theorists, policymakers, and U.S. presidents have contributed their perspectives, and yet, there continue to be as many opinions regarding the purposes of higher education in America as there are stakeholders attempting to achieve them. From a historical perspective, the purposes of higher education have been less concerned with a rigid and esoteric societal role and more responsive to the competing oscillating influences of national events and circumstances, industry and innovation, policy and governance, and innovative technological advances (Harper & Jackson, 2011; Thelin, 2011). More recently, prominent figures have advocated for higher education as a mechanism for achieving specific student outcomes, including the development of communication and critical thinking skills, the building of individual character, necessary preparation for life in a diverse global society, the acquisition of broader individual interests, and successful entry into the world of work (Bok, 2011). For example, although many state governors argue career readiness, job placement, and economic development should be the top priorities, with other purposes lagging far behind, the presidential organization Campus Compact (2015) just asked college and university presidents and chancellors to reaffirm the civic responsibility of higher education in their document *Thirtieth Anniversary Action Statement*. While the three themes of democracy, liberal education, and career readiness are well supported and are differentially convincing options, no one single argument emerges as definitive.

The powerful alignment of leadership education to higher education's missions lies in the fact that across three guiding purposes of higher education (economic development and career readiness, critical thinking and a liberal education, citizenship and an engaged democracy), leadership education is ever-present as relevant and necessary. As a critical behavior for business success, problem solving, or community engagement, developing students' leadership capacities informs and impacts outcomes across higher education's divergent purposes. These sought-after outcomes, whether by employers, scholars, or communities, create the critical demand for the delivery and development of leadership content, skills, and practice in higher education. Chapter 8 will explore how career-based competencies have propelled leadership studies courses and programs in specific disciplines and majors across campuses. While relevant to all three guiding purposes, this chapter argues that we must reclaim our ground in leadership development, which is rooted in the historically relevant and contemporarily salient outcome of higher education's purpose to sustain our democracy.

The guiding principle supporting this discussion of leadership development in higher education is our fundamental belief that we in higher education have a civic purpose that is both implicit and explicit. Senior educational officers and policymakers identify higher education as fundamental to a functioning democracy despite the fact that civic responsibility is neither natural nor effortless (Bok, 2011). This commitment is the result of learning that is specifically structured and implemented to combat the challenges associated with civic apathy and societal decline. Additionally, "college graduates ... will likewise make up the vast majority of all public officials, elected or appointed" (p. 177). These factors begin to reveal the implicit expectation of higher education as an agent of civic education and provide insight as to how we can conceptualize the product of such efforts.

Institutions of higher education produce what can be thought of as a common (or public) good. This argument informs our claim for higher education's purpose in leadership development. We believe that higher education contributes to the betterment of society by preparing individuals for a responsible civic life that has a commitment to social change at its core. The social change required to improve society, however, cannot be accomplished without careful consideration of the knowledge, skills, and values essential to leadership. Thus, the agreement between higher education and the society it serves is characterized by the commitment to produce knowledge, inspire societally sensitive values, and provide the blueprint for the development of leaders and leadership capacity in individuals (Kezar, Chambers, & Burkhardt, 2005).

The outlook that higher education should serve as society's servant and critic requires that higher education be able to serve the needs of those marginalized by society, as well as to alert members of society to the mechanisms by which that marginalization occurs and is perpetuated. For those who have asserted that the purposes of higher education stem from the ability to generate economic activity, our perspective would highlight the ways in which the creation of knowledgeable human capital powers economic growth, as well as the innovation, research, and creativity necessary to drive the economy. Proponents of higher education as the sanctuary of the liberal arts would take solace in the emphasis that our viewpoint places on "engaged learning—learning that emphasizes what students can do with their knowledge ... working to solve significant problems in the larger world" (Schneider, 2005, p. 127). Some have provided a veritable laundry list of

NEW DIRECTIONS FOR HIGHER EDUCATION • DOI: 10.1002/he

outcomes that can be (and in many cases are) associated with higher education. Our perspective, however, amasses these concerns and others within the domain of public engagement, which offers "the principal pathway for intergenerational mobility, strengthened national defense, and [pushed] back the frontiers of knowledge in every dimension of our lives" (Votruba, 2005, p. 263). Therefore, the perspective of higher education serving the public good does not exclude many alternative interpretations of its role and contributions.

This volume welcomes readers from various perspectives on the purpose of higher education: economic development, liberal studies, and community change. As authors, we believe strongly that leadership learning in higher education aligns with and directly impacts students' success in career, life, and community. We also hope that as this chapter and future chapters focus on pedagogy, structures, and outcomes of higher education, readers hear and respond to the call for higher education to purposefully own its unique power and possibility to educate a diverse citizenry prepared to engage and evolve our communities.

## Mission of Higher Education

University and college mission statements play a pivotal role in the power and possibility of leadership programs on our campuses. While institutional mission statements vary, they almost always espouse the traits, outcomes, and/or development of leaders and provide us "license to initiate transformative change and to practice our leadership principles" (Astin & Astin, 2000, p. 93). The conceptualization, articulation, and execution of leadership development programs will vary based on the institutional mission; there are likely to be differences in the programs in public and private universities, 4-year colleges and community colleges, secular and religiously affiliated institutions, and among the various Carnegie families of institutions (Carnegie Foundation for the Advancement of Teaching, 2010). Program development and implementation of mission occur "differently in diverse institutional settings with both intended and unintended consequences that need to be better understood" (Holland, 2005, p. 256). Diverse institutional realities contribute to the richness of higher education, and institution-specific context matters when designing leadership development programs.

All mission statements are not written equally, and specificity can vary in communication of institutional expectations and outcomes. Often mission statements are intentionally vague and are frustrating to interpret in practice. Translating ambiguous statements creates benefits and challenges to leadership programs because the diverse stakeholders across campus will infer differing directives. While research exists linking missions with diversity initiatives (Wilson, Meyer, & McNeal, 2012), service opportunities (Sullivan, Ludden, & Singleton, 2013), and the planning of campus spaces (Fugazzotto, 2009), there is a relative dearth of literature that links institutional mission statements and the presence of leadership education programs on campus. This fact is informative by itself. If leadership education programs were a priority on the agenda of higher education at large, a greater and more robust body of knowledge would exist and more empirical data about outcomes would be available.

In this age of heightened accountability, higher education institutions continue to lack focus on and demonstration of their attainment of student leadership outcomes and the processes that support them, even when the production of societal leaders is a mission-based desired outcome. Mission statements call for student leadership, and yet campuses often assume that proficiency in a discipline automatically translates into effective and efficient leadership training. Not only is this logic misleading, but it is also used as a deterrent to the establishment of leadership education as a discipline unto itself. The lack of collective attention to leadership impacts the capacity of colleges and universities to effectively operationalize their missions in three specific ways: (1) Leadership education can be a misinterpreted element of mission statements, (2) strategic plans may inappropriately operationalize leadership education, and/or (3) leadership education units may not be empowered by their host institutions to implement meaningful leadership education initiatives. Each of these problem situations deserves careful consideration if it is to be overcome.

**Interpretation.**    How college and university faculty, staff, students, and stakeholders interpret institutional policies and procedures significantly affect the daily business of these organizations. Meaning-making processes are at the heart of the college experience, and not just for students. Rituals, symbols, and artifacts in collegiate missions, histories, and environments provide a compass regarding how institutional goals are met. Even when clear messages, supported units, and aligned symbols can be found, there are no guarantees that a campus's objectives will be met. In the more realistic scenario of ambiguous missions, variable support, and chaotic artifacts, success is even more uncertain. Given the detailed and nuanced nature of successful undergraduate leadership education, the interpretation of the institutional mission by those expected to implement that mission is of utmost importance. As the growing field of leadership education attempts to carve a niche of its own, scholars would be well advised to clearly and explicitly define leadership education so that the relationship between it and the mission under which it operates can be clearly understood. For practitioners attempting to utilize leadership education programs, perhaps one of their greatest contributions is contextualizing how their actions fit within interpretations of their institution's mission when teaching, presenting, or writing about their activities. One example of this misinterpretation of mission is explored in Chapter 3, which describes how leadership programs are sometimes designed for only a select and elite group of students. In that situation, leadership educators are most likely misinterpreting their program's mission-based outcomes to focus on only a portion of their

NEW DIRECTIONS FOR HIGHER EDUCATION • DOI: 10.1002/he

students. There are as many ways to interpret an institution's mission as there are individuals attempting to do so; when educators are focused on the role of leadership education in realizing that mission, explicitly articulated interpretations and directly related actions are paramount.

**Operationalization.**    Strategic plans are perhaps the most explicit form of the operationalization, and therefore interpretation, of an institutional mission statement. As formalized documents, they are road maps of how an institution intends to meet its most important goals, and they simultaneously reflect the hierarchy of those goals. For institutions seeking to produce civically responsible student leadership, careful attention must be paid to how a strategic plan takes shape: which goals are selected and how they are organized; who makes decisions and when; where leadership education is situated among those factors; what resources are allocated to make those initiatives successful; who is responsible for carrying out the plans; how goal attainment is measured; and what length of time is afforded for the planning, implementation, revision, refinement, and assessment processes. As higher education continues to operate with nonstandardized inputs, emerging technologies, and differential outputs, the standards for successful strategic plan implementation cannot be measured by the same metrics used in the arenas of business and industry from which they came. However, with thoughtful planning, consistent advocacy, and thorough assessments, successful student leadership education programs can (and in many cases should) be realistic and attainable goals.

**Empowerment.**    Power dynamics in higher education settings can be difficult to understand. Even those individuals who are immersed in such interactions may struggle to find accurate descriptors for the experience. While mission statements and strategic plans may define what should be accomplished, by whom, and why, very rarely do they explicate how. The process by which leadership education programs take shape can be greatly affected by the position of the unit responsible for implementation with respect to institutional power. In cases where leadership education departments enjoy mission-based authority, there is a responsibility to provide opportunities for students that are both congruent to the original sentiment of the mission and to the modern context in which the intended leadership experience operates. There is a delicate balance between teaching leadership to students in the way it might have been intended by the mission and in ways that are relevant to the students' current and future surroundings. When mission-based authority is not present for leadership education programs, the programs may not be constrained by the mission; however, those programs do not benefit from a campus culture that may have developed the kinds of supportive elements that exist in mission-based programs. Authority, however, can come from different sources within an institution of higher education, and although there may be instances in which leadership education is not explicitly articulated as a goal, it may be implied or accomplished in the service of some other stated objective. When leadership is explicitly stated in an institution's mission, there is a categorical imperative for undergraduate leadership development. When leadership is not explicitly stated or implied, we argue that there remains a moral imperative for the successful development and implementation of student leadership education.

Mission statements provide both guidance and guidelines in our understanding of what our institutions of higher education seek to be. Just as we all would critique and judge a person who "talked one way yet walked another," integrity in espoused and practiced values matters. Clarity of the meaning, alignment in strategy, and resources for support guide adherence to institutional missions and can create leadership programs with contextual meaning, structural support, and authority to operate. Khurana and Nohria (2010) challenge college and university educators to recognize this mission–practice gap before students start to ask whether they should even "take the mission statements of the universities they join seriously" (p. 5). This challenge is supported by Guthrie, Bertrand Jones, Osteen, and Hu's (2013, p. 3) question that if higher education institutions continue to say one thing and yet do another, "why should students or society expect or trust colleges and universities to develop the leadership skills necessary for the modern world?"

## Context of Higher Education

More than 15 years ago, the Kellogg Foundation called on institutions of higher education, along with individual faculty, staff, and administrators, to claim their unique responsibility to shape the quality of leadership in our society. The context of higher education is a central player in forming the next generation of leaders through research that defines and guides the practice of leadership, training teachers who educate our citizens, and preparing students for professional careers. In addition to being purpose-driven, leadership development in higher education is contextually relevant. The context of higher education is uniquely designed to develop students' leadership identities and capacities due to its interdisciplinary nature and theory-to-practice learning environment.

**Interdisciplinary.**    The interdisciplinary nature of the collegiate environment allows for the leveraging of multiple approaches to understand leadership education and institutional capacity. Arguably, since their inception, fields such as management and political science have been devising ways to produce individual leaders. Additionally, psychology, sociology, education, and public administration programs have researched the collective ways humans come together to understand and create change. Furthermore, each of these programs and many more have influence, whether in sales, teaching, politics, group behavior, or changing mindsets. A tremendous volume of human capital has been expended in developing, explaining, and creating new bodies of research, models, proofs, and disproofs of leader and leadership knowledge, skills, and values. As a place of idea generation and dissemination, institutions of higher education accommodate a multitude of approaches in attempting to understand leader identity and leadership capacity. Our postsecondary institutions were designed for and retain the capacity to research and develop the concepts and skills of creating change across as many varied disciplines as the number of professions, politicians, and family members attempting to solve wicked problems in their communities. The very nature of the modern college or university is constructed in such a way that those within its walls can leverage a wide range of academic influences to solve adaptive problems. This integration of diverse knowledge, skill, and values makes the prospect of leadership education within a higher education setting more likely to produce effective and efficient results in a shorter time frame with greater utility of resources than any other educational setting.

Across these unique disciplinary silos, higher education in the United States is growing in its skill and responsibility to educate across and between disciplines. Interdisciplinary work—the work of conceptualizing, researching, and teaching a concept from multiple perspectives—is increasing. In addition to interdisciplinary work, student engagement in high-impact, collective learning experiences is driving campus design and budget decisions (Kuh, 2008). In a recent article in *The Atlantic*, Burton (2014) goes so far as to critique this uniquely American collective focus, stating that "insularity seems at odds with the rhetoric of the American educational institution. To be a 'lone wolf,' to simply 'go home and do their homework,' is to neglect, in some sense, a vital component of the educational experienceiple. 3). Burton continues with her assessment that:

> intellectualism alone is not enough, even for an academic institution. Simply learning for learning's sake is not enough. In this paradigm, there is something suspect—even selfish—about a "lone wolf" prospective student that stores up knowledge, like a dragon hoarding treasure. For all that is made of the American tradition of "rugged individualism," American culture is less welcoming to those who neither lead nor follow but simply opt out altogether. (p. 3)

**Theory to Practice.**    Building upon interdisciplinary and engaged ways of knowing, it is the unique theory-to-practice context of higher education that provides a holistic-development environment for young leaders on the college campus. The National Task Force on Civic Learning and Democratic Engagement (2012) describes the benefits of higher education to prepare students to use knowledge and power in responsible ways through actively engaging with the societal, ethical, and practical implications of learning. It is this act of thoughtful engagement, the practice and observation of impact, and the intentionally designed learning environments created by college educators that allow for critical reflection on both successes and failures. At its best, this learning environment is designed in a risk-encouraging, nonjudgmental way where failure as a result of reaching beyond one's current capacity is encouraged and students are picked up, dusted off, and challenged to try again.

As an investment in developing ethical leaders prepared to apply knowledge to societal problems, leadership learning is uniquely aligned with higher education's multidisciplinary resources and practice to try, fail, and try again. Specifically, higher education's use of problem-based learning to teach leadership is explored in Chapter 3, and its focus on critical thinking to solve adaptive challenges is discussed in Chapter 5. Unlike leadership development in a professional context, the various learning environments created by higher education encourage critical reflection on both successes and failures in a nonjudgmental way, allowing for the growth of students and gains in institutional capacity and organizational learning with minimal concerns for profits and losses. Most collegiate environments are a blend of both challenge and support, providing both the obstacles good leadership needs in order to test its mettle but also the resources necessary to develop robust mechanics of success. Describing the higher education context as a "practice field," Chapter 7 explores the many ways students have opportunities to actively engage in learning and failure and to be picked back up to try again on their college campuses.

In higher education, leadership does not have to be expressed as a zero-sum game, and without that pressure, leaders of colleges and universities can encourage innovation and insightful risk-taking, making novel positive developments more likely to occur. Within the context of higher education, we find multidisciplinary expertise, interdisciplinary learning, and a hands-on practice environment for the development of diverse students with leader identities and leadership capacity.

## The Call for Educating Future Leaders

Describing his belief that higher education institutions should educate future leaders, Kellogg president and then-chief executive officer William C. Richardson stated that it "is premised on their role in serving communities and society at large ... it is the role that higher education might play in the greater social environment that inspires our support" (Astin & Astin, 2000, p. vi). He continued by clarifying that leadership education will be a result of institutional commitment and individual role modeling. Students will be the ones who lead us "and they will lead us as we have shown them they should" (Astin & Astin, 2000, p. vi). The call to action implicit in these sentiments is that postsecondary leadership learning environments are materially important to the development of upcoming generations of societal leaders. Higher education must step up to show students, stakeholders, and our communities that we hear and understand the clarion call for better, more distributed, diverse leaders who are actively engaged in making a difference (Astin & Astin, 2000). It was over 15 years ago that Alexander and

NEW DIRECTIONS FOR HIGHER EDUCATION • DOI: 10.1002/he

Helen Astin served as town criers by describing this call and announcing our failures. They wrote, "the concept of leadership and educational goals of leadership development have been given very little attention by most of our institutions of higher learning" (Astin & Astin, 2000, p. 3). Today, we are repeating the call. Higher education has made significant progress since the Astins' report, *Leadership Reconsidered*, and yet we still come up short in our attention to and emphasis on leadership development of all students (Astin & Astin, 2000).

This call is a catalyst to generate conversation focused on higher education's transformative role in leadership education to serve our communities' well-being. Colleges and universities are uniquely poised to address the crisis caused by the lack of abundant leadership in our communities given their unique skill in developing the leadership capacity of young adults (Pascarella & Terenzini, 2005). While honoring the work that has occurred across colleges and universities over the past decade, our hope is for a deeper examination of higher education's role, responsibility, and capacity to educate, develop, and engage the next generation of leaders.

The diversity of student bodies, institutional types, stakeholder needs, and financial resources in the postsecondary landscape should not be taken as an excuse for lethargy in this area. Across missions and types of universities and colleges, the purpose, nature, and mission of higher education call us to educate students to make a difference. Our challenge is to design leadership education programs aligned with institutional culture and resources. The danger of neutrality, of not actively embracing higher education's role in creating leaders for the common good, is that we knowingly perpetuate and exacerbate the social ills that plague our communities (Shriver, 2014).

## Next Steps

Advocates for leadership learning in higher education have resources within their reach to continue the march forward. The first recommendation is to build a knowledge base from which to leverage your institution's particular sense of purpose, mission, and context. In part, the rest of this volume acts to serve as a guidebook for your action. In it, you will find additional recommendations, strategies, and tools that can help you push your campus to not only be clearer about institutional context, mission, and vision, but also about the rituals, symbols, and artifacts used to express the interpretation of these elements. Aligning guiding principles with campus decisions depends on clarity of thought and collaborative action of administrators, faculty, and staff, and this resource is specifically designed to assist you in this alignment.

The second recommendation is to find knowledgeable others to support you wherever they may exist. If you are lucky enough to have a handful of willing and able individuals on your campus, be the spark that ignites the conversation. If not, reach beyond the walls of your institution to neighboring campuses (similar or even rival institutions) and to local, regional, and national conferences. Collaboration is a key component in the development of any program, and its importance cannot be overstated in undergraduate leadership education programs. Not only is the practice of effective leadership collaborative and inclusive of all community voices, but the teaching, developing, and sustaining of leadership programs are also collaborative and inclusive efforts across the rich diversity of campus and community. Leadership is everyone's business and everyone's responsibility in higher education—purposefully, ethically, and uniquely positioned for great strides in higher education.

## References

Astin, A.W., & Astin, H.S. (2000). *Leadership reconsidered: Engaging higher education in social change.* Battle Creek, MI: Kellogg Foundation.

Bok, D. (2011). *Our underachieving colleges: A candid look at how much students learn and why they should be learning more.* Princeton, NJ: Princeton University Press.

Burton, T. I. (2014). *Why are American colleges obsessed with leadership?* Retrieved from http://www.theatlantic.com/education/archive/2014/01/why-are-american-colleges-obsessed-with-leadership/283253/

Campus Compact. (2015). *Thirtieth anniversary action statement.* Retrieved from http://compact.org/resource-posts/presidents-and-chancellors-asked-to-affirm-action-statement-on-public-purposes-of-higher-education/

Carnegie Foundation for the Advancement of Teaching. (2011). *The Carnegie classification of institutions of higher education* (2010 ed.). Menlo Park, CA: Author.

Fugazzotto, S. J. (2009). Mission statements, physical space, and strategy in higher education. *Innovative Higher Education, 34*, 285–298.

Guthrie, K. L., Bertrand Jones, T., Osteen, L., & Hu, S. (2013). *Cultivating leader identity and capacity in students from diverse backgrounds.* ASHE Higher Education Report, 39(4). San Francisco, CA: Jossey-Bass.

Harper, S. R., & Jackson, J. F. L. (Eds.). (2011). *Introduction to American higher education.* New York, NY: Routledge.

Holland, B. A. (2005). Institutional difference in pursuing the public good. In A. J. Kezar, T. C. Chambers, & J. C. Burkhardt (Eds.), *Higher education for the public good: Emerging voices from a national movement* (pp. 235–260). San Francisco, CA: Jossey-Bass.

Kezar, A. J., Chambers, T. C., & Burkhardt, J. C. (Eds.). (2005). *Higher education for the public good: Emerging voices from a national movement.* San Francisco, CA: Jossey-Bass.

Khurana, R., & Nohria, N. (2010). Advancing leadership theory and practice. In N. Nohria & R. Khurana (Eds.), *Handbook of leadership theory and practice* (pp. 3–26). Cambridge, MA: Harvard Business Press.

Kuh, G. (2008). *High-impact educational practices: What they are, who has access to them, and why they matter.* Washington, DC: Association of American Colleges & Universities.

The National Task Force on Civic Learning and Democratic Engagement. (2012). *A crucible moment: College learning and democracy's future.* Washington, DC: Association of American Colleges & Universities.

Pascarella, E. T., & Terenzini, P. T. (2005). *How college affects students: Vol. 2. A third decade of research.* San Francisco, CA: Jossey-Bass.

Schneider, C. G. (2005). Liberal education and the civic engagement gap. In A. J. Kezar, T. C. Chambers, & J. C. Burkhardt (Eds.), *Higher education for the public good: Emerging voices from a national movement* (pp. 127–182). San Francisco, CA: Jossey-Bass.

Shriver, M. (2014). *How a group of women revealed hard truths in higher education.* Retrieved from http://www.nbcnews.com/feature/maria-shriver/how-group-women-revealed-hard-truths-higher-education-n108746

Sullivan, S. C., Ludden, A. B., & Singleton, R. A., Jr. (2013). The impact of institutional mission on student volunteering. *Journal of College Student Development, 54*(5), 511–526.

Thelin, J. R. (2011). *A history of American higher education.* Baltimore, MD: John Hopkins University Press.

Tugend, A. (2012, May 5). Vocation or exploration? Pondering the purpose of college. *The New York Times*, p. B5.

Votruba, J. C. (2005). Leading the engaged institution. In A. J. Kezar, T. C. Chambers, & J. C. Burkhardt (Eds.), *Higher education for the public good: Emerging voices from a national movement* (pp. 263–271). San Francisco, CA: Jossey-Bass.

Wilson, J. L., Meyer, K. A., & McNeal, L. (2012). Mission and diversity statements: What they do and do not say. *Innovative Higher Education, 37*(2), 125–139.

VIVECHKANAND "V" CHUNOO *is a doctoral student in the Higher Education Program at Florida State University.*

LAURA OSTEEN *is the director of the Center for Leadership and Social Change at Florida State University.*

NEW DIRECTIONS FOR HIGHER EDUCATION • DOI: 10.1002/he

**2**

*This chapter focuses on strategies and processes that integrate leadership learning across institutions. It discusses how leadership education fits a liberal education in various institutional types and operationalizes leadership and liberal arts curricula with five competencies.*

# Liberal Arts: Leadership Education in the 21st Century

*Kathy L. Guthrie, Kathleen Callahan*

Since the beginning of higher education in the United States, the liberal arts have been an important part of the curriculum. As purposes have expanded and new institutional types have developed, the philosophy and practice of liberal learning have maintained their pervasiveness. The coupling of liberal arts and leadership education adds a new and needed shift to create the next generation of global leaders. Together, the principles of these formerly separate entities create an integrated learning environment. For the purposes of this chapter, leadership education refers to the curricular and co-curricular opportunities developed for leadership growth, and a liberal education is defined as "an approach to college learning that empowers individuals and prepares them to deal with complexity, diversity, and change" (Association of American Colleges and Universities [AAC&U]; n.d., para 5). Leadership education that uses a liberal arts model emphasizes a broad educational experience and is essential to leadership development (Gardner, 1990). This coupling encourages the development of leaders and citizens with a broad understanding of society. The process of leadership is not inert; it is a dynamic endeavor. Building knowledge, developing skills, and clarifying values are essential to dynamic processes of both leadership education and liberal learning.

## Liberal Arts Curriculum

Through a liberal arts curriculum, students realize the possibilities of human potential (Wren, 2009). It is a course of study designed to prepare individuals to act as citizens and leaders in serving something beyond

New Directions for Higher Education, no. 174, Summer 2016 © 2016 Wiley Periodicals, Inc.
Published online in Wiley Online Library (wileyonlinelibrary.com) • DOI: 10.1002/he.20186

themselves and to live life to its fullest. The terms *liberal arts, liberal studies, liberal learning,* and *liberal education* are often used interchangeably. The term *liberal arts* is used in this chapter, but as our conversation expands, we believe that *liberal studies* or *liberal learning* better characterizes the historical evolution and current place of the liberal arts in the modern curriculum.

**History.**    The Latin interpretation of the word *liberal* translates as "worthy of a free person" (Castle, 1969, p. 59). The liberal arts are subjects and/or skills that are considered essential for a free person to engage actively in civic life. As Wren (2009) explains, liberal arts allow individuals to be truly free and accompany these liberating experiences with learning. While a liberal arts curriculum is grounded in classical education, it is always evolving over time because of the advances in scholarship and changes in societal needs. In the United States, the need for clergy, local leaders, teachers, lawyers, and so on demanded certain curricula in the 17th and 18th centuries at the colonial colleges (Kezar, Chambers, & Burkhardt, 2005). As society changed, higher education's doors opened to both new students and new needs for learning, expanding the definition of liberal education and its place in the modern curriculum.

**Place in Modern Curriculum.**    Advances in scholarship and the demands of the modern world continue to create new challenges for liberal arts curricula. The writing of Frederick Rudolph (1990) is still relevant today. He explained that similar to the liberal arts curriculum, the expansion of extracurricular activities in the 1920s allowed for students to take part in experiences that would prepare them for life after graduation, as these activities place "emphasis on fellowship, on character, on well-roundedness" (p. 464). A current challenge with liberal arts curricula is the increasing specialization within disciplines, which undercuts the integrative nature of a liberal arts education. In addition, institutions of all types have often failed to address the main purpose of liberal arts education: the creation of citizens and leaders. In the mid-1990s, this concern was addressed with the addition of service learning and civic engagement as central components of the liberal arts curriculum. While there are still challenges in implementation, efforts to maintain and increase liberal arts learning across the disciplines and student life are evident on campuses today.

## Leadership Education and Learning Within a Liberal Arts Curriculum

Kellerman (2012) stated that there are over 1,500 definitions and 40 models of leadership. Over the years, the definition of leadership has become more debated than agreed upon. Based on personal experiences, individuals may define this complex concept differently. As a social construct, the concept of leadership holds different meanings to different people (Guthrie, Bertrand Jones, Osteen, & Hu, 2013). Rost (1991) explored the historical development of the word *leadership* and the accompanying definitions in an attempt to develop a definition of leadership that met six criteria: "clear, concise, understandable by scholars and practitioners, researchable, practically relevant, and persuasive" (p. 99). Ultimately, Rost provided the postindustrial definition of leadership that not only undergirds this volume, but also aligns with a liberal arts curriculum because of its focus on relationships. Rost (1991) states, "leadership is an influence relationship among leaders and followers who intend real change that reflects their mutual purposes" (p. 102). Rost's definition of leadership makes it operational at all levels rather than only related to positions of power.

Leadership learning is enhanced through the use of various constructs from multiple perspectives and diverse contexts; it therefore follows that leadership education should be multidisciplinary (Riggio, Ciulla, & Sorenson, 2003). Studying leadership from political, communication, psychological, historical, and sociological perspectives enhances students' understandings of leadership approaches. Exploring these multiple processes and practices of leadership in action is the foundation of effective leadership education programs (Wren, 1994). Structuring leadership education as a multidisciplinary process opens the door to integrating skills and knowledge learned in the liberal arts. The study of liberal arts is fundamentally related to the themes of leadership, and the intentional integration of liberal arts and leadership has the potential to respond to the new challenges confronting modern liberal education. In fact, this integration could be the next shift in liberal arts education.

Liberal arts curricula offer unique possibilities for students to develop reflection and critical thinking skills central to the leadership process. A program that includes both breadth and depth of exposure to other cultures, majors that conclude with critical self-assessments, and interdisciplinary programs that require multidisciplinary perspectives to address ethical and social problems serve to educate students about the vital importance of criticism, context, and connections. As Brown (1994) discusses, a coherent liberal arts curriculum that includes exposure to other cultures allows the liberally educated student to see differently, to see more, and to see holistically. Various perspectives help to create leadership capacity to be responsive to and responsible for discovering meaning and truth in our lives and beliefs. Further, liberal arts curricula are models of self-critical inquiry and openness that complement leadership education's goals of deepening students' responsibility and accountability.

How, though, does the integration of liberal arts and leadership help students succeed after the formal process of higher education has ended? Today, a major topic of conversation is employability. In 2013, the AAC&U sponsored a survey conducted by the Hart Research Associates that shed light on employer priorities for college graduates. A key finding was that "employers prioritize critical thinking, communication, and complex problem-solving skills over a job candidate's major field of study when making hiring decisions" (Hart Research Associates, 2013, p. 4). Employers also preferred students who have both specific knowledge and broad-based liberal arts knowledge. The report states the following:

> There is broad agreement among employers that *all* students, regardless of their chosen field of study, should have educational experiences that teach them about building civic capacity, broad knowledge about the liberal arts and sciences, and cultures outside the United States. (p. 9)

The powerful combination of the purposes of liberal education and of leadership education creates a dynamic learning environment. This research highlights not only the strong connection between the curriculum in leadership education and the liberal arts, but also the importance of the integration of the two.

The Jepson School for Leadership Studies at University of Richmond, through its leadership studies curriculum embedded in the liberal arts, provides one example of how an institution has responded to the need to integrate liberal arts and leadership. The Jepson School was designed to educate future global citizens with the knowledge and skills to become change agents (Jepson School of Leadership Studies, 2007). In the draft proposal written in support of opening this school, the proponents describe a need for "ethical, civic-minded" (p. 3) individuals to take on leadership responsibilities for the future. This definition goes hand in hand with the original purpose of liberal arts. In fact, the goals of the Jepson School mirror a liberal arts purpose including both educating responsible, moral citizens to serve society and broadening students' perspectives.

## Operationalizing the Curriculum: Five Competencies

Examples such as the Jepson School are becoming more common around the United States. With an understanding that the integration of the liberal arts and leadership education is a needed shift for modern curricula, we propose that this integration can be operationalized through five competencies. For the purposes of this chapter, competencies are defined as values, knowledge, abilities (motivations or skills), and behaviors that contribute to one's effectiveness in a role or task (Seemiller, 2013). These five competencies are critical thinking, communication, cross-cultural understanding, ethical capacity, and civic engagement. By using these five competencies, we hope to make a clear connection between liberal arts curricula and leadership education.

**Critical Thinking.**    A liberal education challenges learners to master the skill of critical thinking in order to become civically engaged and well-rounded citizens. Critical thinking transcends specific subject matter and instead examines structures and elements of various concepts that lead to conclusions and implications. The liberal arts operationalize critical thinking by applying it to social issues and civic concerns.

Critical thinking from a leadership perspective entails complex thinking (Flores, Matkin, Burbach, Quinn, & Harding, 2012), which is connected with one of the basic tenants of leadership: cognitive ability (Bass, 1990). In fact, a majority of leadership theories today support the development of cognitive abilities, knowledge, and intellectual stimulation (Northouse, 2013). In an effort to address this need of leaders to develop cognitive ability and complex thinking, many classrooms are turning to critical thinking (Stedman, 2009). Critical thinking is comprised both skill and disposition. While skill is malleable, a critical thinking disposition is one's naturally occurring attitude or preference for critical thinking and is not easily changed. In many instances, there is an assumption that students are different in disposition. However, leadership education offers a unique platform inherently designed to improve critical thinking by cultivating self-regulatory judgment through interpretation, analysis, evaluation, and inference of a leader's own decisions and actions (Facione, 1990), which is able to be developed more than one's disposition.

Leaders deal with complex problems that require complex solutions; thus, leaders who can think critically will be more effective. Leaders also need critical thinking skills that are flexible enough to adapt to rapidly changing environments. While higher education emphasizes critical thinking across disciplines, many undergraduates do not effectively utilize this skill (Burbach, Matkin, & Fritz, 2004). Leadership studies curricula emphasize building skills such as critical thinking through student-centered experiential and active learning (Eich, 2008; Moore, Boyd, & Dooley, 2010). The use of critical thinking skills provides an in-depth and forward-thinking reflection process (Rudd, Baker, & Hoover, 2000). Further, the development of critical thinking capacity allows for a more purposeful and effective reflection process in leadership development (Stedman, 2009). Jenkins and Andenoro provide further examples and a model for critical thinking through leadership education in Chapter 5.

Using as a foundation Ennis's (1993) 10 actions a learner must take to think critically, Jenkins and Cutchens (2011) created 12 actions a leader can take to lead critically. These actions are as follows:

1. Be aware of the context of your situation and evaluate the implications of your decisions.
2. Ask questions and listen appropriately.
3. Take the time to understand the diversity of others' decisions, values, and opinions.
4. Be flexible and open-minded in your decision making.
5. Accept, internalize, and apply constructive criticism.
6. Evaluate assumptions before you try to challenge them.
7. Understand processes before you try to change them.
8. Know the strengths and weaknesses of your followers and direct or empower accordingly.

NEW DIRECTIONS FOR HIGHER EDUCATION • DOI: 10.1002/he

9. Be purposeful and take into account your organization's mission and values when making decisions.
10. Engage others where they are, not where you want them to be.
11. Encourage critical followership.
12. Take informed action. (p. 7)

**Communication.**   As Jenkins and Cutchens (2011) allude to by including different types of communication in their 12 actions as a leader, at the heart of liberal arts and leadership studies is communication; without communication all other actions fail. Skills like critical thinking, cross-cultural collaboration, and achieving the historical qualities of liberal arts of grammar, rhetoric, and logic would be useless without being able to communicate those appropriately to others. Bohm (1996) explained that to *communicate* is to "make something common," from its Latin roots "*commun* and the suffix 'ie' which is similar to 'fie,' in that it means 'to make or to do'" (p. 2). To make something common requires listening, open-mindedness, and the ability to articulate a point of view. Communication calls for these skills in addition to the commonly understood verbal, nonverbal, and written forms. However, when searching liberal arts or leadership studies curricula, our experience has shown that the word *communication* is rarely used. Rather, a leadership studies curriculum is more likely to define a set of skills that are to be developed over time and culminate into the art of communication, both face-to-face and with the use of technology.

Liberal studies and leadership education use an interdisciplinary curriculum as a part of the larger fabric of learning. With the increase of technology and global communications, these skills must be included with the other essential learning outcomes in order to respond to the quick-paced, global environment. The online classroom has become common in higher education, necessitating different knowledge and skills of communication not only for students, but also for faculty and staff. The online global classroom increases cross-cultural interactions as face-to-face communication decreases.

By interacting through multiple means of communication in different environments and through technology, liberal arts and leadership education emphasize the creation of active, global citizens. These global citizens benefit society and not just themselves or their individual communities (Kezar et al., 2005). They are personally and socially responsible, have knowledge of others, and possess intellectual and practical skills, including communication (AAC&U, 2007). AAC&U acknowledged written and oral communication to be essential learning outcomes under intellectual and practical skills within a liberal education (p. 10). This is a small, but key, piece of a larger, more complex puzzle of student learning. These essential learning outcomes put forward by AAC&U must be taught across the curriculum and be practiced throughout students' time in higher education.

NEW DIRECTIONS FOR HIGHER EDUCATION • DOI: 10.1002/he

Examples of communication being used throughout the curriculum are widespread, but one program from the University of Michigan started a movement of dialogue for students. The University of Michigan's Program on Intergroup Relations was started in 1988 and was the first of its kind. When this program was founded, its philosophy was based on helping students manage conflict and improve intergroup relations at a time of racial conflict at the university (for more information, see http://igr.umich.edu /article/igr-history). Intergroup relations instituted intergroup dialogue courses that bring together small groups of students to discuss important issues such as race, gender, nationality, and so on. These are three-credit courses that highlight communication across groups and encourage the importance of communication in managing conflict, establishing community, and better understanding social group identity. Purposefully addressing communication through dialogue with others has the potential to have more impact on students than reading an article or teaching a lesson on communication. Dialogue and communication are at the heart of this program and the many initiatives established over the years. The program is a partnership of student life and the College of Literature, Science, and the Arts. This relationship between academics and the student life staff creates a space for interdisciplinary collaboration. Courses that integrate communication throughout the curriculum, such as those within the University of Michigan's intergroup dialogue program, ensure that students will gain these skills for use in the future.

**Cross-Cultural Understanding.**    The U.S. government began to see the significance of globalization and the need for cross-cultural understanding with the passing of the National Defense Education Act in 1958 (Hunter, 2004). Priorities such as international relations, foreign language, and geography became foci for education and caused a shift in the liberal arts consistent with societal needs. Though at the time this act was a strategic move by the government to increase the knowledge of its citizens, it helped begin a movement for cross-cultural understanding through the curriculum and highlighted the importance of the curriculum in the development of global competence. After World War II, globalization and a commitment to educating a generation of responsible citizens became a part of society, and institutions responded accordingly to adjust their curricula and co-curricula to meet those needs.

To see the importance of cross-cultural understanding in leadership programming, we need look no further than the findings from Dugan and Komives' (2007) multi-institutional study of leadership. They found that engaging students who had differing political opinions or personal values in conversations about sociocultural issues was the strongest environmental predictor of growth in leadership outcomes. Sociocultural conversations included discussions about "different lifestyles, multi-culturalism and diversity, major social issues such as peace, human rights, and justice, and political issues" (pp. 14–15). These findings led Dugan and Komives to provide 10 recommendations for campus leadership programs, including their first recommendation to "discuss socio-cultural issues everywhere" (p. 17). Grounding leadership education in cross-cultural understanding is critical if learners are to demonstrate leadership outcomes.

An example of powerful cross-cultural understanding as a competency of leadership and liberal arts curricula is seen at the U.S. Naval Academy in Annapolis, Maryland. While this institution provides a top liberal education to all students, one central element of that education is an understanding of global and cross-cultural dynamics. As Yu, Disher, and Phillips (2010) discuss, military personnel have to collaborate and cooperate with international partners, which requires a different set of skills. Communicating with and comprehending people who think and behave differently from oneself are critical to understanding complex human interactions. These skills go beyond conflict and are seen more regularly in facilitating disaster relief, peacekeeping efforts, and humanitarian efforts. In addition to critical thinking, communication, and cross-cultural understanding, developing ethical capacity is an important competency in connecting liberal arts curricula and leadership education.

**Ethical Capacity.**    The AAC&U (2007) calls for higher education to commit to "educating responsible and ethical citizens with learning practices" (p. 38). While this call to action is everyone's responsibility, liberal arts frameworks are ideal for engaging students in knowledge development, conversations, and application of personal ethics and individual ethical capacity.

Ethics coursework has been an important part of many leadership education programs (Hackman, Olive, Guzman, & Brunson, 1999). As Ciulla (1998) mentions, leadership programs should cultivate leaders who are both effective and ethical. However, coursework should focus on ethical reasoning and development of ethical capacity, not morals. Morals are static and are at the core of a person's character. Ethics are principles upon which morals are often based. These can be both generally taught in the home or through religious training. However, ethical reasoning—that is, the process of reasoning that increases one's ethical capacity—can be taught (Sternberg, 2010). School is an appropriate place to teach ethics; more specifically, leadership and liberal arts curricula provide opportunities to develop individual ethical capacity and reasoning.

Sternberg (2010) believes case studies are the best way to teach ethical reasoning, and these can be used in coursework and in co-curricular programming to help develop learners' ethical capacities. There is no shortage of case study examples from recent history that relate to ethical issues, including the worldwide financial crash of 2008 and the Enron and Watergate scandals. In addition, there are generic ethical case studies with no easy "right or wrong" isolutions that are designed for use by college students. By utilizing critical thinking and reason, learners can develop skills to navigate situations based in different contexts. The use of case studies gives learners tangible lessons. Utilizing a case study with a new group of selected resident assistants or orientation leaders or in a leadership class can open the door to deep learning and conversation about ethical dilemmas. This also allows for the development of group cohesion, individual and group critical thinking, open dialogue about different issues, and viewing of different perspectives.

**Civic Engagement.**    Kezar et al. (2005) contend that the most recent example of the evolution of liberal arts education is its current focus on civic engagement. Employers have stated their priorities for hiring employees who are engaged in civic life, which has encouraged this shift toward more civic engagement in college. AAC&U (2007) has also acknowledged this movement over the last two decades, specifically in service learning.

Riggio et al. (2003) acknowledged that service learning and experiential education are both key components of a leadership curriculum with a liberal arts format. Courses that encourage service learning and experiential learning put students in real life situations to encourage not only leadership, but also the other competencies of critical thinking, communication, cross-cultural understanding, and ethical capacity. This practice increases students' knowledge, skills, and values in each of these areas over time.

Service learning integrates coursework with service experiences that are tied to a course or an academic field and include reflection and application of learning. These experiences enable students to work in the local community or to travel domestically or internationally to serve different communities or societal needs. One example is at Winthrop University, a public, comprehensive institution in South Carolina where the vice president for student life takes a group of students abroad annually. Prior to leaving, students take part in academic preparation relevant to the country, often through a historical or global leadership lens. Preparation also includes a better understanding of social issues of the country to which students will travel. Students reflect on experiences during and after their trip to apply their learning both in the classroom and through their experience. Opportunities such as service learning that incorporate experiential learning into coursework are just one way to increase awareness of civic engagement and encourage students to contribute to a larger community.

Starting in the fall of 2007, AAC&U's core commitments initiative (Dey & Associates, 2008) surveyed 23 higher education institutions on their campus climate with regard to personal and social responsibility. Findings from this survey align with the need for a liberal arts and leadership education focus. The Civic Learning and Democratic Engagement (CLDE) Program was developed out of the core commitments initiative. Five dimensions in the development of personal and social responsibility emerged from the survey: (1) striving for excellence, (2) cultivating personal and academic integrity, (3) contributing to a larger community, (4) taking seriously the perspectives of others, and (5) developing competence in ethical and moral reasoning. Overall, the researchers found that there was a gap between what students and professionals perceived to be important among these five dimensions and what was actually being done at the institutional level to ensure these outcomes. One interesting finding was that only 33.4% of students believed that after completing college, students should have a stronger or better awareness of the importance of "contributing to a larger community." This finding compares to a larger percentage of students (42.8% or more) who believed they should leave college with better awareness and skills related to the other four dimensions. These findings raise questions about what colleges and universities are doing to increase the percentage of students who believe that contributing to the larger community is of importance.

## Five Competencies Working Together: An Example

The 18-credit Undergraduate Certificate in Leadership Studies at Florida State University boasts an "interdisciplinary, multidimensional, and experiential program" (for more information, see http://thecenter.fsu.edu /Leadership-Studies-Certificate). As stated in the original proposal, the certificate aimed to address knowledge, skills, and values at individual, partnership, group, and community levels. Areas in which students will gain knowledge, skills, and values at the individual level include self-awareness, critical thinking, communication, and visioning/goal setting; at the partnerships level, areas include relationship building, diversity, influence and power, and ethics; at the group level, the areas include group dynamics, organization development, conflict management, and decision making/negotiation; and at the community level, they include systems thinking, social change, civic engagement, and generative leadership. These types of knowledge, skills, and values address each of the five competencies of critical thinking, communication, cross-cultural understanding, ethical capacity, and civic engagement at multiple levels, and students are exposed to these competencies through required and elective courses. The combination of these courses supports the student's learning with an integrated approach of knowledge, skills, and values so that each student will become an empowered leader who intends to make positive change in his or her future community and/or profession.

The certificate is intended to complement a student's major field of study. Students take five required courses along with a sixth course of their own choosing from their major field or an additional course that contributes to their learning of leadership theory (Guthrie & Bovio, 2014). Students from various disciplines engage in the certificate program not only to develop the five competencies mentioned but many others as well. Participation in the program can also enhance their employability after college because it addresses each of AAC&U's employer priorities reported in 2013. This program's success is rooted in its interdisciplinary

**Table 2.1.  Florida State University Undergraduate Certificate in Leadership Studies: Five Competencies and Course Examples**

| Competency | Course Example |
|---|---|
| **Critical thinking** | Students are introduced to critical thinking in LDR 2101: Leadership Theory and Practice. Through learning different leadership theories, students must critically think about their own experiences, understandings, and theories to develop and articulate their own definitions of leadership. |
| **Communication** | In LDR 3215: Leadership and Change, students are exposed to different types of communication and learn about the importance of leadership and communication through change and transition. Students identify a change needed in society, a community, or an organization and must communicate how to apply leadership theory to provide a strategic plan. |
| **Cross-cultural understanding** | In LDR 2231: Global Leadership, students are challenged to think about leadership in a global context. In this course, students develop skills to recognize and analyze differences between individuals and groups, explore global leaders, and distinguish one's own cultural patterns and respond flexibly to multiple worldviews of leadership. |
| **Ethical capacity** | In LDR 4105: Leadership and Complexity, the certificate capstone course, students bring all prior knowledge, skills, and values for application to personal leadership situations. Through ethical capacity building and reflection, students are able to build their own meaning of leadership and their future impact as they graduate and lead beyond college. |
| **Civic engagement** | In LDR 2162: Leadership in Groups and Communities, students are required to fulfill 30 service hours in conjunction with the coursework that includes critical readings on working with groups and creating a lasting impact through the social change model of leadership development (HERI, 1996). |

and cross-curriculum approach. The five competencies give each student a unique and varied tool kit of knowledge, skills, and values to utilize in his or her future (see Table 2.1).

## Conclusion

Connecting liberal arts and leadership education enhances the potential for leadership learning by providing an integrated learning environment. Together, these formerly separate entities result in a needed shift to create the next generation of global leaders. The five proposed competencies complement one another and assist in operationalizing a curriculum that reflects liberal arts and leadership education as demonstrated in the Florida State example. The mastery of critical thinking, communication, cross-cultural understanding, ethical capacity, and civic engagement unites the liberal arts and leadership education curriculum to produce the engaged, global citizens needed for today's world. The shift of focus in the liberal arts over the years is a needed and evolving development for modern curricula. The combining of liberal and leadership education strengthens both of their purposes and sets the stage for students' continued success in the 21st century.

## References

Association of American Colleges and Universities (AAC&U). (2007). *College learning for the new global century* (Report from the National Leadership Council for Liberal Education and America's Promise). Washington, DC: Author.

Association of American Colleges and Universities (AAC&U). (n.d.). *What is a 21st century liberal education?* Retrieved from https://www.aacu.org/leap/what-is-a-liberal-education

Bass, B. (1990). *Bass and Stogdill's handbook of leadership* (3rd ed.). New York, NY: The Free Press.

Bohm, D. (1996). *On dialogue*. New York, NY: Routledge.

Brown, P. C. (1994). Liberal education for leadership. *Liberal Education, 80*(2), 44–48.

Burbach, M. E., Matkin, G. S., & Fritz, S. M. (2004). Teaching critical thinking in an introductory leadership course utilizing active learning strategies: A confirmatory study. *College Student Journal, 38*(3), 482–493.

Castle, E. B. (1969). *Ancient education and today*. Hammondworth, England: Penguin Books.

Ciulla, J. B. (1998). Leadership ethics: Mapping the territory. In J. B. Ciulla (Ed.), *Ethics: The heart of leadership* (pp. 3–26). Westport, CT: Praeger.

Dey, E. L. & Associates. (2008). *Should colleges focus more on personal and social responsibility? Initial findings from campus surveys conducted for the Association of American Colleges and Universities as part of its initiative, core commitments: Educating students for personal and social responsibility*. Washington, DC: Association of American Colleges and Universities.

Dugan, J. P., & Komives, S. R. (2007). *Developing leadership capacity in college students*. College Park, MD: National Clearinghouse for Leadership Programs.

Eich, D. (2008). A grounded theory of high-quality leadership programs: Perspectives from student leadership programs in higher education. *Journal of Leadership & Organizational Studies, 15*(2), 176–187.

Ennis, R. H. (1993). Critical thinking assessment. *Theory into Practice, 32*(3), 179–186.

Facione, P. A. (1990). *The Delphi report*. Millbrae, CA: The California Academic Press.

Flores, K. L., Matkin, G. S., Burbach, M. E., Quinn, C. E., & Harding, H. (2012). Deficient critical thinking skills among college graduates: Implications for leadership. *Educational Philosophy and Theory, 44*(2), 212–230.

Gardner, J. (1990). *On leadership*. New York, NY: The Free Press.

Guthrie, K. L., Bertrand Jones, T., Osteen, L., & Hu, S. (2013). *Cultivating leader identity and capacity in students from diverse backgrounds*. ASHE Higher Education Report, 39(4). San Francisco, CA: Jossey-Bass.

Guthrie, K. L., & Bovio, R. (2014). Undergraduate Certificate in Leadership Studies: An opportunity for seamless learning. *Journal of College and Character, 15*(1), 25–31.

Hackman, M. Z., Olive, T. E., Guzman, N., & Brunson, D. (1999). Ethical considerations in the development of the interdisciplinary leadership studies program. *Journal of Leadership Studies, 6*, 36–48.

Hart Research Associates. (2013). *It takes more than a major: Employer priorities for college learning and student success*. Washington, DC: Author.

Higher Education Research Institute (HERI). (1996). *A social change model of leadership development: Guidebook version III*. College Park, MD: National Clearinghouse for Leadership Programs.

Hunter, W. D. (2004). Got global competency? *International Educator*, 13(2), 6–12.

Jenkins, D. M., & Cutchens, A. B. (2011). Leading critically: A grounded theory of applied critical thinking in leadership studies. *Journal of Leadership Education*, 10(2), 1–21.

Jepson School for Leadership Studies. (2007). *Notes on the founding of Jepson School of Leadership Studies: An abridged draft no. 4*. Retrieved from http://jepson.richmond.edu /about/Draft%20No.%204.pdf

Kellerman, B. (2012). *The end of leadership*. New York, NY: HarperCollins.

Kezar, A. J., Chambers, T. C., & Burkhardt, J. C. (2005). *Higher education for the public good: Emerging voices from a national movement*. San Francisco, CA: Jossey-Bass.

Moore, C., Boyd, B. L., & Dooley, K. E. (2010). The effects of experiential learning with an emphasis on reflective writing on deep-level processing of leadership students. *Journal of Leadership Education*, 9(1), 36–52.

Northouse, P. (2013). *Leadership: Theory and practice* (6th ed.). Thousand Oaks, CA: Sage.

Riggio, R. E., Ciulla, J. B., & Sorenson, G. J. (2003). Leadership education at the undergraduate level: A liberal arts approach to leadership development. In S. E. Murphy & R. E. Riggio (Eds.), *The future of leadership development* (pp. 223–236). Mahwah, NJ: Erlbaum.

Rost, J. C. (1991). *Leadership for the twenty-first century*. Westport, CN: Praeger.

Rudd, R., Baker, M., & Hoover, T. (2000). Undergraduate agriculture student learning styles and critical thinking abilities: Is there a relationship? *Journal of Agricultural Education*, 41(3), 2–12.

Rudolph, F. (1990). *The American college and university: A history* (2nd ed.). Athens: The University of Georgia Press.

Seemiller, C. (2013). *The student leadership competencies guidebook*. San Francisco, CA: Jossey-Bass.

Stedman, N. L. P. (2009). Casting the net of critical thinking: A look into the collegiate leadership classroom. *Journal of Leadership Education*, 7(3), 201–218.

Sternberg, R. J. (2010). Teaching for ethical reasoning in liberal education. *Liberal Education*, 96(3), 32–37.

Wren, J. T. (1994). Teaching leadership: The art of the possible. *Journal of Leadership Studies*, 1, 75–93.

Wren, J. T. (2009). Reinventing the liberal arts through leadership. In J. T. Wren, R. E. Riggio, & M. A. Genovese (Eds.), *Leadership and the liberal arts: Achieving the promise of a liberal education* (pp. 13–36). New York, NY: Palgrave Macmillan.

Yu, M. M., Disher, T., & Phillips, A. T. (2010). Educating warriors: Globally engaged and culturally aware. *Liberal Education*, 96(2), 22–29.

KATHY L. GUTHRIE *is an associate professor in higher education and coordinator of the Undergraduate Certificate in Leadership Studies at Florida State University.*

KATHLEEN CALLAHAN *is a lecturer in the Leadership and American Studies Program at Christopher Newport University.*

**3**

*This chapter explores problem-based learning (PBL) as effective pedagogy to enhance leadership learning. Through institutional examples, research, and personal experiences, the authors provide a rationale for faculty and staff to utilize PBL across the curriculum.*

# Creating Problem-Based Leadership Learning Across the Curriculum

*Sara E. Thompson, Richard A. Couto*

This chapter explores problem-based learning (PBL) in college teaching and student development. We suggest that the challenge of educators, both inside and outside the classroom, is to facilitate problem-based learning for students because of its efficacy in teaching, learning, and moral development. We suggest also that by increasing problem-based learning, we become more deliberate and intentional about creating deep leadership learning (Astin & Astin, 2000; Roberts, 2007). Consequently, this chapter explains problem-based approaches in leadership learning, their effectiveness, and ideas for creating PBL across the curriculum. In order to model what we are discussing, this chapter adopts a reflective-practice approach, treating leadership development as a problem and problem-based learning as a pedagogy to address that problem. Only then does it make sense to discuss ways to create PBL across the curriculum.

## Moral and Leadership Development

The first, but most often overlooked, question of creating any form of leadership development is what is being developed. The path of leadership definitions is well travelled with hundreds of definitions and paved with tome upon tome. However, most of these definitions explicitly or implicitly conflate leadership and authority. This presents a particularly acute problem for the leadership development of undergraduate students. What authority do they have? Some may be officers in campus organizations, but to cater to this group suggests that leadership relates to an elite group and not to everyone. As presented in Chapter 1, college mission statements often

New Directions for Higher Education, no. 174, Summer 2016 © 2016 Wiley Periodicals, Inc.
Published online in Wiley Online Library (wileyonlinelibrary.com) • DOI: 10.1002/he.20187

talk about imparting a passion for ethical leadership and civic responsibility in *all* students, not just the officers of student organizations. Leadership development for college students requires a definition of leadership apart from formal positional authority. Grounded in the postindustrial philosophical frame discussed in the Editors' Notes, we offer this inclusive, reasonable, and relevant definition: Leadership is taking initiative for shared values and the common good. This definition separates leadership from the position of authority—the "leader"—and places emphasis on the act of leading. When we approach leadership as an action rather than a position, the problem of leadership development seems to be how we develop people who are willing to take initiative for shared values and the common good.

Building upon that definition of and approach to leadership, the problem of leadership development becomes clearer. Research shows that college students are exploring their own moral development through a variety of cultural, intellectual, and social activities (Kohlberg, 1981; Pascarella & Terenzini, 1991; Rest, 1986). As young adults, they are formulating their values and balancing their thoughts of personal and common good. Students are navigating between what they, as individuals, will gain or lose in various forms of the common good and considering whether their own societal norms are shared communal values (Kohlberg, 1981; Rest, 1986). This context of our work with young adult learners underscores the wisdom of addressing their leadership development through a moral development lens. Those of us in leadership programs at the college level, like it or not, are dealing with the moral development of young adults (Day, Harrison, & Halpin, 2008; Kegan & Lahey, 2009 c).

## Problem-Based Learning as a Leadership Pedagogy

As a pedagogy that addresses the intersection of moral and cognitive development, PBL is an effective method for promoting the leadership development of students. Defined broadly, *problem-based learning* engages the learner in a situation or problem that requires him or her to recall information from an existing knowledge base and connect the situation to personal challenges, experiences, and/or self-reflection (Barrows & Bennett, 1972; Hmelo-Silver, 2004; Yeo, 2007). Through PBL, students are gaining important skills that differ drastically from memorizing information in traditional ways. They work collaboratively with other students through defined steps: identifying the problem, researching information, sharing this newfound knowledge with others, and making decisions or recommendations to solve the problem. These steps also resemble leadership in action, at least leadership as adaptive work (Heifetz, 1998). Many other pedagogical approaches, such as self-directed learning, service-learning, experiential learning, action-based learning, and small group work, share these characteristics of PBL.

The starting point of PBL, whatever its form, is to create an in-depth, memorable learning experience that will help students learn about themselves. In its approach, PBL intentionally enhances and integrates personal learning and academic learning to help students reach explicit understandings about themselves. The assumption we are making is that this knowledge brings students better insight into their values, their views of the common good, and who shares them.

PBL is recommended not only because of these outcomes, but also because its process requires the conflict and collaboration inherent in leadership as we have defined it. PBL challenges us as educators both inside and outside of the classroom to shift our mental models from teaching to learning, from methods to purpose, and from a distinction of moral or cognitive development to the bond between them. This means transforming a classroom or workshop format into an environment where students can take responsibility for their own learning. Of course, any success resulting from PBL belongs to the students and their willingness to take responsibility to deal with the problem set before them.

For example, at the University of Illinois Leadership Center, staff created a leadership program, called Ignite, that gave students a campus or community problem and asked them to interact with the client to solve the problem. This scenario included numerous PBL methods such as asking questions, creating concept maps, working in a group, critical thinking, and reflection. Not all examples of PBL are interpersonal and external, however. At Claremont McKenna College in the foundational leadership theory course, I (Thompson) help students address intrapersonal dimensions of leadership. They identify organizations or groups that they are passionate about and in which they are actively engaged outside the classroom. Then, throughout the semester, they reflect on their experiences with these groups. By asking questions and responding to their personal journal entries, I make the learning personal and encourage students to incorporate these lessons into their learning and living environments (Guthrie & Thompson, 2010).

Participatory action research, defined as a collaborative process between researchers and the people who are expected to benefit from the research (Chevalier & Buckles, 2013), shows the amazing power of PBL. The most exciting moment of my (Couto) teaching experience was the day I arrived in my class later than usual and the 15 students in my class had started without me. It was mid-semester and midway through a participatory action research project on diversity at the university. The students had chosen and shaped the topic, and they were conducting research on it. With neither time nor need to wait for a teacher to arrive to say they could start, the students began working on the tasks that they knew very well they had to do. From that time to the very successful conclusion of the study, the project was a shared responsibility.

NEW DIRECTIONS FOR HIGHER EDUCATION • DOI: 10.1002/he

In my (Couto) experience at the University of Richmond, I also saw the way that participatory action research can play a part in leadership curricula. In one of the very first classes at the university's Jepson School of Leadership Studies, students created a charter of commitment. In this charter, students examined the extent of community service at the university by interviewing faculty, student group leaders, administrators, and staff. Subsequent classes took on campus problems such as binge drinking and, with the direction of community partners, off-campus problems such as breast cancer. This approach transformed the classroom into a community with a common purpose and provided all members of that community the chance to give their personal gifts to the process.

## Leadership Learning Beyond the Classroom

These magic learning and development moments also happen outside of the classroom in co-curricular environments where students are removed from their day-to-day surroundings and are given the opportunity to engage with others in day-long or multiday retreats. Through self-reflection and personal work, students are able to use these retreat experiences to transform parts of their lives and to reach their fuller potential.

Jonathan comes to mind, I (Thompson) met Jonathan when, as a high school student, he attended a week-long leadership program. I subsequently had a personal coaching relationship with him throughout his college years. During his time in college, he started to explore how he could take his unique gifts as a relationship-oriented engineer and share them with the world. After winning competitions for innovation and entrepreneurship in 2010, Jonathan started his own nonprofit organization, the Illini Prosthetics Team (IPT), to build prosthetic limbs for people in underdeveloped countries at a reasonable cost.

Throughout this journey, Jonathan applied key examples of PBL to his leadership learning. First, he had a cause (or a problem) that drew him to accomplish greatness for others (i.e., 2 million people in the world living without limbs). Through deep personal reflection and experience, he recognized the satisfaction he felt when helping others—specifically his grandmother, who had limited use of her hand. He decided he wanted to use his gifts to create change in the world. Creating affordable prosthetic limbs provided him an opportunity to learn by doing; to ask challenging questions of himself and those around him (small group collaboration); to look for guidance from mentors when being challenged beyond his limit; to apply his leadership learning to real-life problems (self-directed learnings); and then to grapple with the successes and the shortcomings of these experiences. Through self-reflection and feedback, Jonathan wrestled with questions about his own leadership style, learning limits, and finding the right people to join his team and then developing his approach to working with these teammates to design, develop, and deliver prosthetic limbs to people who needed them.

Eventually, he transferred his position as president of the nonprofit organization to one of his colleagues in order to move to Guatemala and work on the ground with the amputees IPT has helped. Jonathan's passion and purpose were to help people, and through deep reflection he was able to let go of the prestige associated with being the founder of this organization and shift his role to actions that were more meaningful to him.

## PBL Across the Curriculum

The methods of PBL are less important than its fundamental purpose: building a community of deep learning. From our observation, often because of an overly structured curriculum, many instructors tend to overlook profoundly important aspects for deep learning; educators in outside-the-classroom settings can be flexible and engage students on these finer points. For example, in-class instructors might leave it to chance for class participants to learn each other's names—an important step in creating community. I (Couto) always made sure that in my classes of 20 to 30, students could identify each other by name. Although learning each other's names took extra time, I found that the process built community.

Simple steps such as knowing each other's names require being deliberate and intentional in leadership development efforts across the curriculum. Instructors can become overwhelmed with the enormity of their task and forget simple, yet important and essential, components. Perhaps the first simple step in creating PBL across the curriculum is to recognize that it already goes on in our students' lives. If we are fortunate enough, students may ask us to help them learn from an existing problem or make something we say or do meaningful beyond our intent. The college years are a prime time for students to explore their identities and engage in new experiences to understand their values, passions, and purposes in life. Our work can have a life-changing impact on our students, but often that impact occurs without our knowing it. Most college or university instructors can probably recall having a past or present student confide that something the instructor said touched the student personally and profoundly. As gratifying as that might be, if we are honest with ourselves, we often cannot remember making such a statement, and sometimes we doubt that we did. Our solace in these instances is that by using PBL practices, we deliberately created an environment in which students could hear ideas important to them regardless of our actual words.

Occasionally, in the co-curricular environment, I (Thompson) struggle to frame these PBL opportunities because I am so focused on connecting each experience to a community-based organization or a social justice cause. In these moments, I remind myself it need not be complicated, however important it may be. If I shift my mental frame slightly to meet students where they are, I find numerous opportunities to use PBL to deepen a student's leadership experience. For example, I sent a group of 11 female students to a women's leadership conference and framed this experience with a preconference meeting. In this meeting, students created leader development plans and identified tangible learning goals such as developing self-confidence, building and sustaining relationships with a certain number of people, and practicing being more assertive in social situations. By having this preconference meeting, I was able to better understand each student and craft my follow-up conversations with each of them. The women shared these personal goals and helped each other work toward their respective goals. Upon their return, students shared their progress on individual goals and as a group identified ways to use the momentum from this experience to positively influence what they perceived to be a chauvinistic campus culture. In this example, students engaged in reflection and critical thinking around a personal challenge and then garnered support from a peer group.

Student impACT, a student organization at Claremont McKenna College, works to create opportunities for students to engage in and learn about social innovation within the college and campus communities. A 4-hour workshop designed by Student impACT focuses on deepening the understanding of each person's talents and strengths. In a workshop held in 2013, participants identified the challenges associated with new, small work teams in their respective organizations and discussed how to create structures that support the goals of the organization by building on each person's unique strengths. Students identified opportunities to incorporate these reflections into functional operations of their organizations. Workshop participants were developing critical thinking skills and reevaluating existing systemic mechanisms to identify nuances that are relevant as they developed new concept maps that connected leadership and social innovation in their student organizations.

Another example of leadership development at Claremont McKenna College is the Innovative Start-Up Award, a competition in which students compete in one of two tracks, either a social venture track or a commercial venture track. The award for each winner is $12,500 in prize money that he or she can use to start a business. There are multiple stages in this competition, including an initial round in which approximately 30 teams of students are narrowed to 8 teams (four social-track teams and four commercial-track teams). Workshops are then offered to all of the teams to deepen their learning about various areas of hard business skills, innovation, change, and leadership; one area in particular is working effectively in teams. Students attend this workshop with their peers, identify the challenges they are currently experiencing in working as a team, and assess the various work styles that exist in their team. Students then incorporate their learning by discussing ways to work more effectively as a team. Through reflecting on prior experiences, students are combining a number of learning approaches, such as asking good questions, exchanging feedback, and applying the knowledge acquired in the workshop to improve the way the team is functioning. Staff members work diligently to provide students with feedback throughout the process, to encourage campus-wide participation in workshops when it is feasible, and to engage in dialogue with students about the learning opportunities at the conclusion of the program. Given the competitive nature of activity, this emphasis on learning and development counteracts the tendency to focus only on the end goal of winning the cash prize and better guarantees that every team gains something from the experience.

## Institutional Support

As with any pedagogical shift, institutional support is critical. The examples we have provided of creating successful PBL opportunities across the curriculum include simple one-on-one formats, classroom and co-curricular activities, and campus-wide programs that have become a part of the instructional infrastructure. However, these opportunities would not occur without institutional support.

We believe there are three important reasons that institutions should support the use of PBL across the curriculum. First, when leadership development is mentioned either explicitly or implicitly in the mission statement of every college and university, PBL is an unspoken, but shared, value that is worthy of tangible support. Second, faculty and staff are eager to excel in teaching and welcome effective pedagogies if they have assistance. At the University of Richmond, my (Couto) own experience in providing faculty assistance with PBL was highly rewarding. A survey of teaching practices conducted at the university showed an inverse relationship between faculty members' views of effective pedagogies and what actually happened in the classroom. Lecture was seen as the least effective and most often used form of pedagogy, while forms of experiential education were seen as most effective and least often used! We found that instructors welcomed the opportunity to integrate PBL into their syllabi if their learning curves were gradual, not steep, and if they had assistance with the logistics.

The third reason institutions should support PBL is that it works. Few pedagogies or activities do more to promote the missions of our colleges and universities. If mission statements are to be more than bromides, they need to be expressed in action. In this chapter, we have used some anecdotes to illustrate the impact and importance of PBL on the cognitive, moral, and leadership development of students. But we also can cite extensive quantitative and aggregate evidence of the effectiveness of PBL and the related pedagogy, such as service learning, across fields of study (Bridges & Hallinger, 1995; Eyler & Giles, 1999; Yeo, 2007).

## Characteristics of PBL That Encourage Deep Learning

We know the key characteristics that are important to PBL's success as a tool for deep learning (Eyler & Giles, 1999). PBL begins with the presentation of a problem that builds on existing knowledge and includes a component of challenge that will stretch the learner and encourage him or her to engage in active learning (Wood, 2004). Wood describes the difference between deep learning and surface-level or shallow learning. Shallow learning occurs when students are asked to memorize or listen to a lecture and take notes. However, strategies of deep learning provide opportunities for students to digest new information and actively engage in experiential learning, requiring each student to add this new knowledge to his or her conceptual frame. Many cognitive psychologists highlight how we learn from experience, engage in the learning process, and add to our knowledge base from the interactions that transpire in experiential situations (Wood, 2004).

Typically, in problem-based learning experiences, students have a problem to solve, work in small groups with the guidance of a facilitator, use scaffolds—teaching tools—to support their learning, and engage in self-directed learning (Schmidt, Rotgans, & Yew, 2011). Saye and Brush (2002) describe these tools as *soft scaffolding,* defined as teacher support, or *hard scaffolding,* defined as handouts or worksheets. The goal with these teaching tools is for the students to incorporate the knowledge into their long-term memories, so that they no longer need these scaffolds or teaching aides. When students in small groups collaborate with others, they also engage in peer-to-peer teaching. A facilitator, sometimes called a *tutor* in the PBL literature, assists in challenging students in the learning process and adding value through additional content information or process interventions that ensure effective communication and group functioning (Schmidt et al., 2011).

Last, students engage in self-directed learning, which encourages them to take ownership for and regulate their own learning. Schmidt et al. (2011) describe students who use PBL strategies as being more likely to engage in learning outside of the curricular or co-curricular experience. These authors are describing the students who come to our offices looking for more—more opportunities to learn, to engage, to grow. Cronin (1995) describes them as students of leadership "who have more to give, no matter how much they have given" (p. 32).

In addition to this research, our reflection as authors on our combined 50 years of practice suggests that no matter the form or venue of PBL is, its effectiveness increases when the following occur:

- The stakes of the student action are real—someone needs what the student is providing whether tutoring, prosthetics, or health services.
- The student has a knowledgeable partner who provides insight into the underlying conditions that surface in the symptoms of the problem.

- There is sustained student-to-student or student-to-faculty interaction.
- There is enough time for the student's efforts to have an impact.
- The students have time to reflect on the work that they do.

## Conclusion

We have discussed PBL as a particularly useful tool for the moral and leadership development of young adults. We have eschewed the notion of leadership bound to position and authority in favor of the notion of leadership as a process or initiative taken on behalf of values and the common good. We have provided a definition broad enough to include service learning, action research, and other forms of experiential, problem-centered pedagogies. As we have shown, abundant evidence exists for the efficacy of these pedagogies in promoting the moral, cognitive, and leadership development of students. All of this provides a rational basis for creating problem-based learning across the curriculum.

While necessary, such a rational basis is not sufficient. Creating problem-based learning across the curriculum involves the leadership it promotes and the process that makes it effective and rewarding. Leadership of faculty and staff, with and without positions of authority, is required to take initiative on behalf of the shared values and common good that problem-based learning serves. Magical moments of impact for us as teachers will increase if we are deliberate and intentional about creating opportunities for students to engage in the process of leadership (i.e., problem solving) and if we talk less about collaboration and create more spaces for students to collaborate in PBL and to find out more about themselves in that process. As educators, the process of creating PBL learning environments is extremely rewarding; we witness transformational learning experiences that feed the soul, connect us to the students, and remind us of the importance of blending learning and moral development across the curriculum.

## References

Astin, A.W., & Astin, H.S. (2000). *Leadership reconsidered: Engaging higher education in social change.* Battle Creek, MI: W. K. Kellogg Foundation.

Barrows, H. S., & Bennett, K. (1972). The diagnostic (problem solving) skill of the neurologist: Experimental studies and their implications for neurological training. *Archives of Neurology, 26*(3), 273–277.

Bridges, E. M., & Hallinger, P. (1995). *Implementing problem based learning in leadership development.* Portland, OR: Eric Clearinghouse on Educational Management.

Chevalier, J. M., & Buckles, D. J. (2013). *Participatory action research: Theory and methods for engaged inquiry.* London, England: Routledge.

Cronin, T. E. (1995). Thinking and learning about leadership. In J. T. Wren (Ed.), *The leader's companion: Insights on leadership through the ages* (pp. 27–32). New York, NY: The Free Press.

Day, D. V., Harrison, M. M., & Halpin S. M. (2008). *An integrative approach to leader development: Connecting adult development, identity, and expertise.* New York, NY: Psychology Press.

Eyler, J., & Giles, D. E. (1999). *Where is the learning in service-learning?* San Francisco, CA: Jossey-Bass.

Guthrie, K. L., & Thompson, S. (2010). Creating meaningful environments for leadership education. *Journal of Leadership Education, 9*(2), 50–57. Retrieved from http://www.fhsu.edu/jole/

Heifetz, R. A. (1998). Adaptive work. In G. R. Hickman (Ed.), *Leading organizations: Perspectives for a new era* (2nd ed.). Thousand Oaks, CA: Sage.

Hmelo-Silver, C. E. (2004). Problem-based learning: What and how do students learn? *Educational Psychology Review, 16*(3), 235–266.

Kegan, R., & Lahey, L. L. (2009). *Immunity to change: How to overcome it and unlock potential in yourself and your organization.* Boston, MA: Harvard Business Press.

Kohlberg, L. (1981). *Essays on moral development: The philosophy of moral development* (Vol. 1). New York, NY: Harper & Row.

Pascarella, E. T., & Terenzini, P. T. (1991). *How college affects students: Findings and insights from twenty years of research.* San Francisco, CA: Jossey-Bass.

Rest, J. R. (1986). *Moral development: Advances in research and theory.* New York, NY: Praeger.

Roberts, D. C. (2007). *Deeper learning in leadership: Helping college students find the potential within.* San Francisco, CA: Wiley.

Saye, J. W., & Brush, T. (2002). Scaffolding critical reasoning about history and social issues in multimedia-supported learning environments. *Educational Technology Research and Development, 50*(3), 77–97. doi:10.1007/BF02505026

Schmidt, H. G., Rotgans, J. I., & Yew, E. H. (2011). The process of problem-based learning: What works and why. *Medical Education, 45*(8), 792–806.

Wood, E. J. (2004). Problem-based learning: Exploiting knowledge of how people learn to promote effective learning. *Bioscience Education e-Journal, 3*(5), 5–17.

Yeo, R. K. (2007). Problem-based learning: A viable approach in leadership development? *Journal of Management Development, 26*(9), 874–894.

SARA E. THOMPSON *is the director of leadership programs at the Kravis Leadership Institute at Claremont McKenna College, where she is focused on leader development of college students through teaching and experiential learning programs.*

RICHARD A. COUTO *is a senior scholar at Union Institute and University.*

4

*This chapter focuses on how the application of critical pedagogy to leadership education allows for issues of identity, power, and culture to shape the process of leadership learning. Examples from the authors' work with various populations of students of color are used to illustrate critical leadership pedagogy.*

# Critical Leadership Pedagogy: Engaging Power, Identity, and Culture in Leadership Education for College Students of Color

*Vijay Pendakur, Sara C. Furr*

In 2009, Ospina and Foldy conducted a critical review of race and ethnicity in leadership literature and found a startling gap in the extant scholarship: studies that connect a critical, collective understanding of race and ethnicity to the phenomenon of leadership development. They write that these rare, intersectional approaches to leadership research

> aim to explore the rich cultural milieus where collective meanings of race-ethnicity, largely influenced by structures of power, play a significant role in shaping leadership. They illuminate how the constraints imposed by race-ethnicity are transformed into individual and collective resources that can be used in the work of leadership to shape meanings, representations and even power relations. By doing so, these studies implicitly emphasize the collective dimensions of leadership. (p. 887)

Ospina and Foldy note that this gap is not limited to research studies but also persists in leadership development practice in higher education. Much of the current literature does not provide insight as to *how* faculty and staff acquire the knowledge, skills, and attitudes necessary to engage in personal reflection on one's own identity, recognize social systems, and understand how identity shapes the development of cross-cultural relationships. We contend that critical pedagogy can be a useful tool for higher education professionals to examine how identity impacts their work with students in and outside the classroom. As higher education continues to

NEW DIRECTIONS FOR HIGHER EDUCATION, no. 174, Summer 2016 © 2016 Wiley Periodicals, Inc.
Published online in Wiley Online Library (wileyonlinelibrary.com) • DOI: 10.1002/he.20188

deepen its commitment to diversity and social justice, leadership education is also a rapidly growing focus at many colleges and universities. Faculty and staff are continually developing new pedagogy and curricula to help college students understand their values as leaders, develop a sense of what leadership looks like for themselves, and learn socially responsible applications of leadership and critical pedagogy, thereby bridging the aims of diversity education with the praxis of leadership education.

This chapter is designed to introduce critical pedagogy, and its utility, to higher education professionals as they develop leadership pedagogy and curricula specifically for students of color. The first section emerges from Vijay Pendakur's work with Asian American college students and takes a specific look at utilizing critical race theory, a form of critical pedagogy, to help students of color develop a racially empowered leader identity. The second section comes from Sara Furr's work with a first-year retention program for students of color and outlines ways to infuse critical pedagogy into the popular social change model of leadership development (Astin, 1996; Cilente, 2009) to make it relevant and effective for racially marginalized student populations.

## What Is Critical Pedagogy?

Critical pedagogy is a body of writing that attempts to apply the tenets of critical theory to classroom and co-curricular teaching. It enables scholars to explore connections between the fundamental objects of analysis in critical theory—ideology, power, and culture—with frameworks for application and practice, namely curriculum and pedagogy (Nesbit, 2004). From a critical pedagogical perspective, Freire (1970) proposed that in a critical classroom, the experience of the students becomes central. In the critical cultural approach to learning, the link between power, knowledge, language, and identity is essential in the learning process (Fenwick, 2003). A primary goal of those that apply critical theory to practice is to create inclusive spaces. Therefore, from the critical perspective, learning involves a process of addressing power, challenging assumptions, creating a space for honest and authentic dialogue, increasing critical reflection and thinking opportunities, and bringing all perspectives together to create a more inclusive setting (Brookfield, 1993).

## How Can We Use Critical Pedagogy as a Tool?

We define pedagogy to include the teaching methods one employs as well as the curriculum and philosophy that undergird one's practices. Our broad definition of pedagogy is inclusive of faculty teaching in the classroom, outside-of-class interactions with higher education professionals across the college or university (e.g., academic advisors, admissions officers, student affairs professionals), and experiences such as problem-based learning.

NEW DIRECTIONS FOR HIGHER EDUCATION • DOI: 10.1002/he

Critical pedagogy prompts all members of the campus community to consider issues of power and ask questions, such as whose voices are heard and whose voices are not, in the process of making decisions related to students' learning. Critical pedagogy pushes educators to not only consider curriculum, philosophies, and teaching approaches, but also to consider the kinds of power relationships that are maintained by their decisions, as well as what inequities need to be challenged in the process of making pedagogical decisions. When applied to leadership education, critical pedagogy opens possibilities for faculty and staff to work more effectively with various communities of students of color by centering issues of race, power, and identity as foundational to developing empowered leader identities. The next two sections of this chapter offer examples from the authors' work experience to illustrate how critical pedagogy can enhance the outcomes of leadership education with two different groups of college students. The first example utilizes critical race theory to illicit counterstories of the Asian American college student experience, and the second example utilizes the social change model of leadership development as a tool for both developing programs and tending to issues of race and power in a peer-to-peer mentoring program for students of color.

**Vijay Pendakur's Example: Leader Identity, Critical Race Theory, and Asian American College Students.**    *A memory lingers like oil on the surface of my mind. As an undergraduate student, I studied Japanese at a large public institution in the upper Midwest. At the end of my freshman year, I was cramming for finals with a group of other Japanese majors and my study buddy, Susan, said to me, "You know, I'm going to be transferring and not returning here in the fall. I wanted to let you know that you speak so well." I was flattered and a little shocked that Susan wasn't going to return to campus in the fall, so I stammered back, "Uh, thanks. I actually didn't think my Japanese was that great." She replied, "No, I was talking about your English." I smiled weakly, fumbled with my pen, and said nothing back.*

*Shocked. That's all I can remember feeling on the walk back to my residence hall from the library. Slowly, the numbing silence of shock receded, uncovering anger and hurt. I recall getting off the elevator on my residence hall floor and heading straight over to my friend Bill's room. Bill, a White guy from a northern suburb of Chicago, had been my friend for most of my freshman year. I told Bill the story, exclaiming, "I can't believe she thinks that I'm not American! I mean, listen to the way I speak!" Bill was angry for me. He shook his head and said, "Hey bro, I just want to let you know, I totally think of you as White." He put his hand on my shoulder and gave me a comforting squeeze.*

Stories like this are peppered throughout my adolescent and collegiate years. My parents are immigrants from India, and I grew up in a primarily Black neighborhood at the northern border of Chicago trying to understand who I was using a Black–White racial binary. Clearly, as an Asian American, this binary did not serve me well. Upon heading off to a large state school for college, I assumed that my identity journey would somehow become

NEW DIRECTIONS FOR HIGHER EDUCATION • DOI: 10.1002/he

less turbulent and that clear markers would emerge to guide me as I came to understand what it means to be Asian in America. Frequent encounters with Susan and Bill–type situations left me reeling and confused; how could I be inscrutably foreign and comfortably White at the same time?

I open this section of the chapter with a personal anecdote not simply to share something common in the Asian American experience, but to offer an example of the difference between a story and a counterstory. Critical pedagogy contends that if we can shape these types of stories into counterstories, we can form a radicalized sense of our racial selves that offers a stronger foundation for leadership development (Ladson-Billings & Tate, 1995). My first experience with Susan and Bill gave me a story, but I did not possess the knowledge or capacity to recast it into an empowering counterstory at that time. As I learned and grew into identifying consciously as Asian American, I was able to harness my racialized experiences as counterstories, and these served as a foundation for my development as a leader.

Critical race theory (CRT) asserts that racism is endemic in American society, and for CRT in the field of education, this fact calls for a focus on how racism legally, culturally, and psychologically limits opportunities for students of color (Tate, 1997). Tate also sharply questions epistemic claims of "neutrality, objectivity, color blindness, and meritocracy" (p. 235) and calls for educators to problematize research and pedagogy that adhere to these flawed constructs because they serve as veils for dominant interests. In parallel with rejecting classic academic notions of objectivity and neutrality, CRT centralizes stories, and the act of storytelling, in unearthing the lived experience of people of color. Ladson-Billings and Tate (1995) explain that not only are stories themselves important, but the act of counterstorytelling can also serve as "medicine to heal the wounds of pain caused by racial oppression" (p. 57). Finally, CRT asserts that history and context are crucial to addressing the experiences of people of color. In educational praxis and educational research, this final challenge is a reminder to us that we must not ignore the crucial role of history in shaping our understanding and experience of race, as well as the integral nature of class, gender, and other social identities.

CRT challenges us to recognize the importance of race in the lives of college students, help them develop a critical understanding of the roles of history and power in shaping their racialized experiences, and support them in developing counterstories to both challenge oppression and heal the psychic wounds caused by racism. In the last decade, I have worked as a student affairs practitioner and a faculty member, and I am often called on to work with Asian American college students as they develop their capacities as leaders. Using CRT, I've developed a workshop curriculum and pedagogy that help these emerging leaders harness their lived experiences to generate counterstories that serve as a foundation for leader identity development.

I've found my first task to be simply exposing these students to the often hidden history of the Asian American experience, dating back to the

1830s. Over the years, I've collected dozens of images of Asian Americans throughout U.S. history dating back to the late 19th century, and I use these images in concert with quotations from historical texts to expose students to the collective Asian American counterstory. I ground this sprawling historical tale in three key pillars of Asian American racial formation: perpetual foreignness, model minority status, and problematic panethnicity (Alvarez, 2002; Junn, 2007; Kim, 2012; Ng, Lee, & Pak, 2007). The critical literature on Asian American racial identity cites these three tropes as central organizing principles on which the Asian American racial experience, including a history of racial oppression, has been built.

As the historical counterstory approaches the present, I am intentional about including numerous present-day examples of how canonical racial stereotypes continue to haunt the Asian American experience, such as the images of fortune cookies on the Jumbotron at Madison Square Garden during Jeremy Lin's hot streak in basketball (Hadley, 2012), or the stream of Twitter vitriol after two Indian American kids won the National Spelling Bee and dozens of tweets emerged asking questions such as "Why can't the spelling bee championship go to an American?" (Bever, 2014). I then offer workshop participants a quote like "Asian Americans are made, not born," and I ask them, "What experiences have made you?"

Many leadership-education pedagogies involve helping emerging leaders identify the life experiences that have produced their values, commitments, or even fears. Critical pedagogy challenges us to use these same techniques in parallel with the reality that Asian American college students are often experiencing race and racism, but they are often unable to articulate these formative elements in their lives (Alvarez, 2002; Kim, 2012). By priming learners with a critical historical counternarrative, the seminal question "What experiences have made you?" can produce deep reflection and introspection. When they have been properly supported, I have witnessed many Asian American college students beginning to identify what critical race theorists would call *counterstories*. For these students, counterstories are vital to the development of a racially salient leader identity.

I have also collected dozens of images, quotes, and stories of Asian American historical resistance, organizing, and agitation. I share these stories with my workshop participants to illustrate a second counterstory of activism and empowerment to accompany the history of oppression. I conclude this portion of the workshop with the question "How do you make yourself?" Racial identity development is both a process of understanding how macro structures shape our experience of life *and* how each of us possesses agency and capacity for resistance. By exposing learners to dual counterstories of oppression and resistance, I hope to galvanize a sense of conscious leadership in which Asian American leaders understand how they have been shaped by their racial context and their own agency of their lived commitments. This type of workshop can offer Asian American students a foundational race-conscious leader identity that can then be built upon throughout their collegiate journeys in varied leadership education settings.

Much like the students that I've worked with in the past 12 years, my own journey mimicked this process of developing a race-conscious leader identity that then allowed me to grow broadly as a leader. In the years that followed my freshman encounters with Susan and Bill, I proceeded to take courses in Asian American Studies, American history, and East Asian studies. I also went on to have many more personal experiences with racism and White privilege. Feelings of anger, hurt, shock, and shame were fed and shaped in the crucible of collegiate life, but I emerged from the academy with a growing vocabulary to name my experience of race. While in college, calling myself Asian American gave me strength and pride to endure and challenge pervasive racism. Being Asian American connected me to a legacy of antiracist, anticolonial resistance that is an integral part of the American story. Searching for other Asian Americans led me into the campus multicultural center, where I made close friends, became an engaged student leader, and eventually had my first encounters with student affairs, my chosen profession. Through learning and reflection, I was able to take my stories and make them counterstories that continue to fuel and support my work as a leader and educator today.

**Sara Furr's Example: The Social Change Model of Leadership Development and College Students of Color.**    *Coming out of high school, I knew leadership. I was president of the honor society, captain of the cheerleading squad, and a senior class officer. I knew how to get elected, how to lead people, and how to work with other leaders. I knew leadership as positions to attain, hold, and from which to lead others within organizations. This is what it meant to be a leader: being willing to step up and do more work than others.*

*Then I went to college. For the first year I avoided all involvement except for a few cultural student organizations before finally joining Students for Change (SFC). The group was marketed as a cross-cultural coalition, and I didn't really know what that meant. When I walked into the classroom, I experienced the most racially diverse group I had seen at the university. My regular classes weren't this diverse. The mix of body hues represented in the room enthralled me; I spent the first half of the meeting looking around in awe without really paying attention to what was being said. After I started paying attention, I was even more confused. Who was in charge? This was unidentifiable.*

*We gave our names at the beginning of the meeting, and each time students spoke, they would restate their names, but the rest of the meeting was spent throwing out various issues students were experiencing on campus, in their classes, or in the city. Someone was making a list on the chalkboard as different people spoke. As this part of the meeting died down, someone else said that we needed to make a list of skills and knowledge we wanted to gain this year. I kept wondering who the president was and whether there was an agenda. At this time, I became frustrated: Shouldn't one of the leaders be telling us what our focus should be and the corresponding skills or knowledge we need to achieve the* groups' goals? Isn't that their job as leaders? I left the meeting unsure whether I would return. However, I did return, and this would be the start of my journey as an activist and change agent.

As an organization, SFC employed a flat structure, with individuals taking the lead on the projects they brought to the group and each person having equal voice in deciding what we needed to address and what sort of action was required. It was empowering and inclusive and in some ways devoid of the challenges we were addressing in our community. Prior to becoming involved in SFC and becoming an activist, my leadership journey had been focused on me as an individual and had very minimal connection to community, directly or generally. It wasn't until well after graduate school that I realized I had experienced leadership in action: the social change model of leadership development. It not only helped me connect and make meaning of all of my experiences, but also forced me to be more intentional about providing explicit opportunities for traditionally marginalized students, like myself.

## Critical Pedagogy and the Social Change Model of Leadership Development

Created in the early 1990s in response to the gap in leadership literature, the social change model of leadership development (SCM) was the first framework directed toward understanding leadership among college students (Astin, 1996; Cilente, 2009). The model focuses specifically on understanding leadership development, thus leadership as a process, not just as a concept or a study of leaders. While it is quite comprehensive, there are a few areas in which the SCM can be enhanced. In its discussion of individual and group values, it does not name or acknowledge how social identities such as race, gender, class, and so forth affect one's understanding of values or access to them, thus leaving out the varied experiences of students of color in particular. Infusing critical pedagogy in the reading, understanding, and utilization of the SCM provides an understanding of how the specific values are realized and the context for group values in the SCM. Critical pedagogy offered me an opportunity to utilize the SCM as a diversity-mentoring tool.

The SCM is about leadership for social change, which is important to note because one must first understand social identity and structure before creating social change. The SCM describes the relationship between individuals, groups, and communities, specifying seven values each one should be striving for individually and collectively, with change situated directly in the middle of their interactions (Cilente, 2009). The SCM defines consciousness of self, congruence, and commitment as the values on which individuals should focus, but it does not articulate or expand on how to do this. The model also does not address the way social identity impacts these values. For example, consciousness of self requires "an awareness of personal beliefs, values, attitudes, and emotions" (Cilente, 2009, p. 54),

NEW DIRECTIONS FOR HIGHER EDUCATION • DOI: 10.1002/he

and congruence requires a person to act in accordance with those beliefs, values, attitudes, and emotions. However, people of color are not always able to behave in congruence with their personal beliefs, values, attitudes, or emotions because they are not always valued in society. In addition, the ways in which people of color understand their identities are impacted by sociohistorical factors.

Infusing social identity within the SCM allows practitioners to utilize it within the program development of a peer-to-peer mentoring program and the training of peer mentors. Activities that allow students to name their social identities (e.g., race, class, gender, sexual orientation, and religion) and the salience of their identities enable them to situate themselves within the overall program or initiative. A helpful guiding question is "Who am I?" In my work in diversity mentoring, I utilized activities and training opportunities to explore dominant and subordinated identities, helping students recognize how social identities are related to ideas of privilege and oppression and gain a more comprehensive understanding of the individual within the SCM. Experiences that allow mentors to know themselves aid them in building authentic relationships with their mentees that are based on trust. Ultimately, these experiences allow new students opportunities to share their individual stories and become more comfortable with themselves and their identities.

The social change model calls groups to come together with common purpose, engage in collaboration, and embrace controversy with civility. These three group values support group effectiveness in leadership, as I described in my opening story. Collaborative relationships provide an opportunity for multiple perspectives, but only if the group allows differing ones, while controversy with civility provides a way to work through conflict that can arise from differing perspectives, requiring "thoughtful and considered difference of opinion to be heard within a group" (Cilente, 2009, p. 60). Without the presence of this value, the discomfort of conflict silences individuals. Infusing critical pedagogy in understanding the group's values leads me to ask, "Do all individuals have the same access to groups?" and "Who defines civility?"

A training activity focused on building relationships across difference can help student leaders understand controversy with civility. During the activity, it is important to allow mentors to brainstorm potential challenges they may encounter while developing cross-cultural relationships and then offer the group a chance to role-play ways to mitigate or move through those challenges. Time can be spent engaging students in discussion about stereotypes or biases they hold, where/how they gathered that information, and how it impacts their behavior or relationships. To help students embrace a common purpose, it is important to build in time for the group to set team expectations, develop methods of group accountability, and respond to questions such as these: What does civility look like for them? As individuals in this group or community (peer mentors), how do they want to hold each other accountable? Does everyone agree? This is another activity that develops deeper investment in not only the program but also one another, and it helps instill a sense of responsibility to holding one another accountable.

Change and community are the last elements of the SCM. Change is the ultimate goal and is situated in the middle of individual, group, and community values. In the peer-to-peer-mentoring example, the desired social change is increased retention of first-year students of color. From day one, mentors learn that this is the primary goal of the program, and with each training opportunity or activity, they discuss and further understand how different components of the program contribute to this larger goal. Community provides an overall context to understand the various program components and the primary value, which is citizenship. The SCM defines citizenship specifically as individuals seeing themselves as part of a larger whole. College students in particular exist within several communities at one time, simultaneously occupying the campus community, their neighborhoods or geographic communities, their families, perhaps student organizations or groups, and more. Explicitly providing students with the opportunity to understand their multiple communities and the roles they play within them rounds out the use of SCM as a diversity-mentoring tool. Two helpful guiding questions are "Who are we in a community?" and "How do I want to contribute to social change?"

The final day or set of training activities can incorporate both community and change. Activities that build onto previous activities and integrate previous components of SCM allow student leaders to develop a comprehensive understanding of self, others, and community. As discussed in chapter 3, off-site problem-based learning experiences can allow students to integrate their learning. Some options include visiting a challenge course or doing a day of service. While these opportunities typically focus on various tasks, sometimes physical, focused reflection helps students relate their experiences to themselves and their leadership roles. The key to integrating experiences such as these lies in the focused reflection opportunities. Therefore, it is very important to ask students to make explicit connections to previous activities and learning.

## Conclusion

Ospina and Foldy (2009) write:

> In research on leadership, the experiences of people of color are often treated as a special case, rather than as the potential source for theorizing from within a particularly important social context, given the pervasiveness and impact of race in social experience. ... We suggest that the field can—and must—learn from leadership studies that focus on race–ethnicity as particularly rich contexts within which insights about the human condition as it pertains to leadership can be gained. (p. 877)

In this chapter, we have attempted to heed Ospina and Foldy's suggestions and provide two different *rich experiential contexts* from our work as higher education professionals to produce insights that can further the aims of leadership education. We see critical pedagogy as a powerful bridge between the extant approaches to leadership development and the racialized realities of college students of color. Critical pedagogy can help us develop curricula that are relevant to the lived experiences of race and racism for many college students of color, as well as produce leader identities that are grounded in an empowered sense of self. Furthermore, critical pedagogy can be applied to existing, canonical leadership models, such as the social change model, to help in meaningfully including social identities, such as race or sexual orientation, which are at the heart of students' leadership learning.

Finally, critical pedagogy can help us make real the promise of diversity and inclusivity that is at the heart of the academic enterprise by meaningfully including all marginalized group members in leadership education. While the tangible examples from this chapter focused explicitly on students of color and on racial identity, critical pedagogy can be easily applied across numerous social identity contexts, such as gender, sexual orientation, or ability status. Critical leadership pedagogy can open new possibilities for full inclusion of these marginalized group members, and this, in turn, will transform our curricula and practices as the field of leadership education continues to evolve.

## References

Alvarez, A. N. (2002). Racial identity and Asian Americans: Supports and challenges. In M. K. McEwen, C. M. Kodama, A. N. Alvarez, C. Liang, & S. Lee (Eds.), *New directions for student services: No 97. Working with Asian American students* (pp. 33–44). San Francisco, CA: Jossey-Bass.

Astin, H. S. (1996). Leadership for social change. *About Campus, 1*(3), 4–10.

Bever, L. (2014). *Scripps National Spelling Bee draws racially charged comments after Indian Americans win again.* Retrieved from http://www.washingtonpost.com/news/morning-mix/wp/2014/05/30/scripps-national-spelling-bee-draws-racially-charged-comments-after-indian-americans-win-again/?tid=pm_national_pop

Brookfield, S. (1993). Self-directed learning, political clarity, and the critical practice of adult education. *Adult Education Quarterly, 43*(4), 227–242.

Cilente, K. (2009). An overview of the social change model of leadership development. In S. Komives et al. (Eds.), *Leadership for a better world: Understanding the social change model of leadership development* (pp. 43–78). San Francisco, CA: Jossey-Bass.

Fenwick, T. J. (2003). *Learning through experience: Troubling orthodoxies and intersecting questions.* Malabar, FL: Krieger.

Freire, P. (1970). *Pedagogy of the oppressed.* New York, NY: Continuum International.

Hadley, F. (2012). *Jeremy Lin row reveals deep-seated racism against Asian Americans.* Retrieved from http://www.theguardian.com/commentisfree/cifamerica/2012/feb/21/jeremy-lin-racism-asian-americans

Junn, J. (2007). From coolie to model minority: U.S. immigration policy and the construction of racial identity. *Du Bois Review, 4*(2), 355–373.

Kim, J. (2012). Asian American racial identity development theory. In C. Wijeyesinghe & B. W. Jackson (Eds.), *New perspectives on racial identity development: A theoretical and practical anthology* (2nd ed., pp. 138–160). New York, NY: NYU Press.
Ladson-Billings, G., & Tate, W. F., IV. (1995). Toward a critical race theory of education. *Teachers College Record, 97*(1), 47–68.
Nesbit, T. (2004). Class and teaching. In R. St. Clair & J. Sandlin (Eds.), *New directions for adult and continuing Education: No. 102. Promoting critical practice in adult education* (pp. 15–24). San Francisco, CA: Jossey-Bass.
Ng, J. C., Lee, S. S., & Pak, Y. K. (2007). Contesting the model minority and perpetual foreigner stereotypes: A critical review of literature on Asian Americans in education. *Review of Research in Education, 31*(1), 95–130.
Ospina, S., & Foldy, E. (2009). A critical review of race and ethnicity in the leadership literature: Surfacing context, power and the collective dimensions of leadership. *The Leadership Quarterly, 20*(6), 876–896.
Tate, W. F., IV. (1997). Critical race theory and education: History, theory, and implications. *Review of Research in Education, 22*(1), 195–247.

VIJAY PENDAKUR *is an associate vice president of student affairs at California State University, Fullerton.*

SARA C. FURR *is the director of the Center for Inter-Cultural Programs at DePaul University.*

5

*This chapter provides the critical leadership logic model as a tool to help educators develop leadership-learning opportunities. This proactive logic model includes curricular and co-curricular educational experiences to ensure critical thinking through leadership education.*

# Developing Critical Thinking Through Leadership Education

*Daniel M. Jenkins, Anthony C. Andenoro*

In the movie *Dead Poets Society*, the character John Keating, played by Robin Williams, commented, "I always thought the idea of education was to learn to think for yourself." This statement identifies one side of an ongoing struggle within education, a struggle that pits the idea of depositing knowledge into learners' heads so they can do well on exams against building capacity for depth of thought and complex adaptive problem solving. The challenges that face our world are becoming increasingly complex, forcing leaders to leap beyond previously conceived solutions and develop innovative processes and procedures. The ability of leaders to address the crises amid economic struggles, competitive markets, cultural and social adversity, and countless other factors will be critical for the sustainability and advancement of organizations and communities. "The task of leading during a sustained crisis—whether you are the CEO of a major corporation or a manager heading up an impromptu company initiative—is treacherous" (Heifetz, Grashow, & Linsky, 2009, p. 62). Often those with decision-making power attempt to implement technical solutions to address these challenges. While they can be can be useful during short periods of organizational practice, technical solutions often ignore the adaptive complexity that is required to create sustainable solutions (Yukl & Mashud, 2010). In response, flexible and adaptive leadership is becoming a critical piece of the leadership landscape as managers and administrators attempt to keep up with the pace of change that affects today's organizations (Burke & Cooper, 2004; Dess & Picken, 2000). Critical thinking is an essential component of the decision-making process that includes systems perspectives and produces adaptive solutions for real and sustainable organizational and community change. Therefore, it must be a prominent fixture within the higher education landscape.

NEW DIRECTIONS FOR HIGHER EDUCATION, no. 174, Summer 2016 © 2016 Wiley Periodicals, Inc.
Published online in Wiley Online Library (wileyonlinelibrary.com) • DOI: 10.1002/he.20189

The problem with this assertion is that the needs of our society far outweigh the capacity of higher education. Learners in higher education are at a deficit when it comes to addressing adaptive challenges. As faculty, we observe learners who arrive with a willingness to learn, and yet the educational opportunities presented to them provide an overload of content that prevents critical application. Further, time constraints make it difficult for instructors to delve into the complexity and systems perspectives that are necessary for developing adaptive solutions. This situation, coupled with an overwhelming amount of content and assessments of mastery focused on multiple-choice exams, provides considerable challenges for learners and may lead to biased and uninformed perspectives. This pedagogical stalemate requires a new educational paradigm that focuses on the inclusion of critical thinking applied within adaptive contexts to the authentic challenges that face today's world. Chapter 2 addresses critical thinking as a core competency linking leadership education and the liberal arts, but how can critical thinking be included in a new educational paradigm?

In an effort to address this shift and promote the development of the next echelon of leaders, countless academic and student development programs have begun prioritizing the development of critical-thinking skills and dispositions in their learners in the hope that they will create a foundation for sound leadership practice. However, the definitions, programmatic initiatives, and methodologies surrounding the development of these skills and dispositions vary considerably. This merits the consideration of a focused and intentional trajectory that creates process-oriented outcomes for the fusion of leadership and critical thinking education.

Grounded in the work that informs our understanding of critical thinking, we provide a process logic model (see Figure 5.1) that addresses key

### Figure 5.1. Critical Leadership Logic Model

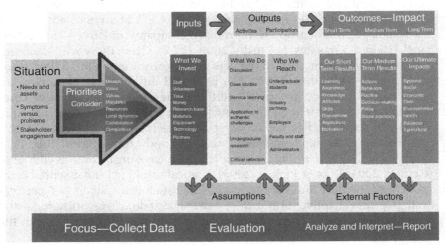

considerations for building a context that empowers critical thinking and engagement in today's learners. To establish a foundation for the model, it is important to consider the roots of critical thinking. Prior to 1990, much of the literature devoted to understanding critical thinking was focused on skills and skill development. This focus contributed to a superficial view of critical thinking that limited its characterization as an assortment of skills rather than as a complex intentional process that aids individuals in making reasoned and judicious decisions (Paul & Binker, 1990). In 1994, Peter and Nancy Facione provided an important addition to the scholarship on critical thinking, aligning the previously identified skills with disposition. Their understanding of the intersection between skill and disposition is highly transferable to leadership education contexts. Facione and Facione (1994) define critical thinking as follows:

> purposeful, self regulatory judgment which results in the interpretation, analysis, evaluation, and inference as well as the explanation of the evidential, conceptual, methodological, criteriological, or contextual considerations upon which judgment is based. (p. 2)

The definition's distinctive connection between disposition and skill provided a more holistic understanding of critical thinking than prior definitions and has received considerable attention in recent decades as academics attempt to create a foundation for the development of related skills and dispositions within leadership contexts (Facione & Facione, 1994; Halpern, 2002; Stedman & Andenoro, 2007). Ennis (1993) also defined critical thinking as "reasonable reflective thinking focused on deciding what to believe or do" (p. 2). Ennis's use of the word *or* is an important evolution because it suggests action (doing) versus simple beliefs (thought).

Through the development of critical thinking skills and dispositions, student and academic affairs professionals, faculty, and countless others who work in dynamic learning contexts can create a foundation for a variety of the necessary competencies linked to successful leadership. Moore and Parker (2012) identify critical thinking as the foundation for reasoning, developing arguments, examining doubts, communicating effectively through written and oral forms, establishing credibility, problem solving, and creating a moral foundation for practice. These skills are essential for successful leaders and align with what employers are looking for. Employers value both skill and disposition (Halpern, 1996), making them essential to higher education and vocational preparation (Stedman & Andenoro, 2007). Further, the case has been made that educating learners to be critical thinkers is vital for society in general (Kennedy, Fisher, & Ennis, 1991; Sternberg, 1985). Those who become critical thinkers acquire such intellectual resources as background knowledge, operational knowledge of appropriate standards, knowledge of key concepts, possession of effective heuristics, and certain vital habits of mind (Bailin, Case, Coombs, & Daniels, 1999).

NEW DIRECTIONS FOR HIGHER EDUCATION • DOI: 10.1002/he

Critical race theory and critical pedagogy, as referenced in Chapter 4, are examples of how these skills can be utilized in leadership and leadership education.

## An Innovative Approach to Critical Thinking Within Leadership Education Contexts

Leadership education is the pedagogical practice of facilitating leadership learning in an effort to build human capacity and is informed by leadership theory and research. It values, and is inclusive of, both curricular and co-curricular educational contexts (Andenoro et al., 2013). Yet, only recently has critical thinking integration in postsecondary leadership education been documented (e.g., Burbach, Matkin, & Fritz, 2004; Jenkins & Cutchens, 2011). Nonetheless, the interdisciplinary contexts of leadership programs are ripe grounds for the aforementioned transcendent approach to critical thinking integration. One advantage is that the approach "prompts greater appreciation of the importance of *how* one thinks about different types of problems and solutions" (University of Southern Maine, Lewiston-Auburn College, 2013, p. 6). No matter the discipline or context for teaching, "the point of getting learners to think critically is to get them to recognize, and question, the assumptions that determine how knowledge in that discipline is recognized as legitimate" (Brookfield, 2012, p. 28). According to Jenkins and Dugan (2013), an interdisciplinary approach to leadership promotes application across contexts, exposure to multiple ideas, and the recognition of situational influences, such as what leadership looks like across disciplines. This approach allows for a variety of streams of critical thinking pedagogy, such as borrowing best practices from multiple disciplines and integrating them within a shared language of leadership. Thus, it is the responsibility of instructors to facilitate this conscious integration.

In the same way, educators, administrators, and practitioners often attempt to apply theories and perspectives within a wide range of contexts. While this can be effective for some contexts, it can actually be a detriment for others. This provides the impetus for critical reflection. Leadership educators in various contexts should reevaluate the percentage of time devoted to conveying and discussing information on leadership versus the time spent by participants reflecting on their own situations and applying tools to help them successfully navigate those situations (Conger, 2013). The logic model we provide in Figure 5.1 and the accompanying narrative illustrate a proactive process oriented to develop critical thinking and leadership capacity in undergraduate learners. This forms a foundation for adaptive leadership practice and sustainable organizational and community change. Further, educators, administrators, and practitioners can use the model to create valuable leadership-learning opportunities for the learners they serve.

## The Critical Leadership Logic Model

The logic model progresses from left to right, examining the various elements influencing the development of critical thinking through leadership-learning opportunities. For the practical purposes of this description, educators, administrators, and practitioners will be referred to as *instructors*. Before attempting to construct any leadership-learning opportunities, it is important to consider the situational influences that impact the learning environment. These institutional factors set the foundation for understanding why the priorities of the learning opportunity have importance. The priorities arrow asks the instructor to consider the institutional constructs that provide parameters for creation of the leadership-learning opportunities. The model then follows an input (what we need), output (what will we see), and outcome/impact (demonstrated results) format. The inputs area of the model then transitions to the outputs area, which is comprised of activities (what we aspire to do) and participation (who we aspire to reach). Accordingly, the inputs and outputs take into account the assumptions of the learners and instructor as identified by the assumptions box beneath the sections. Finally, the outcomes and impacts are influenced by external factors.

**Situation.**    Context is critical. A learner who possesses a superficial understanding of the systems impacting a given situation is predisposed to making superficial decisions about that situation. These superficial decisions often lead to superficial outcomes and a lack of sustainability. Thus, it is absolutely critical to consider the situational factors within a given context, as noted by the arrow on the left side of the model. In his model of integrated course design, Fink (2013) suggests identifying the situational factors that influence decisions about educating learners with respect to learning goals, teaching and learning activities, and feedback and assessment. These factors include, but are not limited to, the context of the class, learners, meeting modality, the nature of the subject, and the characteristics of the learners and teacher. Similar to problem-based learning, described in Chapter 3, learners must connect each of the aforementioned factors to their own contexts and experiences to come to new knowledge and conclusions.

An example of this can be seen within the idea of critical leadership. *Critical leadership* refers to a call for instructors to bridge, integrate, and facilitate the gaps between critical thinking and action for learners in leadership programs (Jenkins & Cutchens, 2011). Yet, a current gap exists that limits the transcendence of leadership learning across knowledge, experience, practice, and application. Conger (2013) describes three critical shortcomings that limit classroom experiences in leadership education and impede the facilitation and transfer of useful learning and its application to the day-to-day challenges that leaders face: (1) the reality gap, (2) the skill-intensive gap, and (3) the application gap. "Many of our leadership constructs fail to identify leadership as a process that is highly contingent and multidirectional; instead focusing on models or approaches that offer 'what ifs' versus actual action" (Conger, 1992, p. 30). Moreover, educational experiences need to reinforce the necessity of "situation reading" skills (Conger, 2013, p. 80), provide opportunities for learners to apply critical-thinking skills to leadership decisions and actions (Jenkins & Cutchens, 2011), and connect theory and practice.

**Inputs.**    Inputs ask the instructor to consider what a learner should invest in the learning opportunity. This often-overlooked piece ensures that the leadership activities, lessons, or programs will be sustainable. Decisions about these inputs should involve multiple stakeholders and account for the context characteristics of the learners and instructors in each learning environment (see Fink, 2013). Instructors in curricular and co-curricular contexts invest time, money and materials, and often staff, volunteers, and institutional or community partners into their learning environments. Moreover, they are compiling knowledge resources and making epistemological decisions about the content of their leadership programs, choosing from textbooks, articles, and videos; websites; and workbooks, to name just a few. Through this process, they are assembling the essential inputs required to facilitate critical leadership learning.

**Outputs.**    Outputs ask the instructor to consider what the learners will see, do, or experience in the learning that occurs. The activities section provides facilitated activities that create opportunities to develop critical thinking skills and dispositions in the leadership learners. Specific learning activities engage learners in critical thinking activities aimed at creating a foundation for the development of real solutions for authentic challenges. The participation section lists specific participants that are critical to the leadership-learning process. Inclusive participation demonstrates an integrated approach to learning that prioritizes diverse perspectives, systems thinking, and application to real-world contexts.

According to Harvey and Jenkins (2014), knowledge, praxis, and reflection are the three critical elements in leadership programs, regardless of the discipline, college, program, or department facilitating the learning. Arguably, pedagogies that intentionally integrate critical thinking across these three elements will have the greatest influence on the development of learners' critical thinking dispositions and skills. A focus on knowledge (or inputs, within the tripartite model) would provide opportunities for learners to challenge assumptions, theories, models, and approaches. Perhaps pedagogy is the bridge to practice (or praxis), just as critical leadership bridges thinking with action.

Dr. Martin Luther King, Jr., noted that "the function of education is to teach one to think intensively and to think critically" (Hobbs, 2010, para 1). For instructors, facilitating practice opportunities in and out of class in which learners can apply critical thinking to leadership situations is a critical challenge. While not comprehensive, discussion, case studies and method, problem-based learning (see Chapter 3), and critical reflection pedagogies may provide learning environments conducive to teaching critical thinking in leadership contexts.

**Outcomes—Impact.**    Assessment and evaluation of programmatic and educational experiences are critical to our understanding of how we can strengthen and create curricula to better develop future generations of leaders. This is affirmed by the outcomes and impact portion of the model as it provides an answer to the question "leadership for what?" This section asks the instructor to identify short-, medium-, and long-term outcomes that can be demonstrated by the leadership learners. Short-term results focus on the development of skills and dispositions, while medium-term results focus on the actions and behaviors that stem from the short-term results. Finally, instructors focus on the ultimate impact of their efforts, addressing systemic and institutional impacts and shifts. This piece of the model creates opportunities for formative (ongoing solicitation and analysis of feedback/data during a given educational experience) and summative (evaluation of perspectives or performance compared against a benchmark measure at the end of a given educational experience) measures. However, this also provides an opportunity for developmental evaluation. Developmental evaluation goes beyond formative and summative evaluation by "supporting innovation development to guide adaptation to emergent and dynamic realities in complex environments" (Patton, 2010, p. 1). This becomes critical to understand as leaders and educators are faced with adaptive challenges within contexts rich with complex variables. Functionally, developmental evaluation identifies and frames a set of educational opportunities that are responsive to a particular situation and are aimed at eliciting a given outcome (Patton, 2010). Essentially, it is a process that defines and codifies the process resulting in leadership.

## Strategies for Developing Critical Thinking Skills and Dispositions

Leadership educators focus a significant component of their work on helping students become strong critical thinkers. Three salient strategies—discussion, case studies, and critical reflection—are practical ways for students to develop critical thinking skills and dispositions.

**Discussion.**    According to Cross (2002), discussion is uniquely designed to encourage learners to strengthen their intellectual muscles and practice their strategic learning moves. Thus, it is important to note that discussion-based pedagogies are the most frequently used in leadership education (see Jenkins, 2012, 2013). Yet, experts agree that leading a productive discussion is among the most challenging and demanding tasks of an instructor—and one of the most satisfying when things go well (Cross, 2002). Thus, it is imperative that leadership educators facilitate discussions that are intentional and, perhaps even more so, critical. According to

Brookfield (2012), to make discussion critical, facilitators should: (a) focus on members identifying assumptions, (b) focus on the degree to which these assumptions are accurate and valid, (c) attempt to fix the contextual validity of assumptions, (d) uncover evidence for generalizations, (e) keep a record of the links in an "inferential chain," (f) generate multiple perspectives, and (g) be alert for groupthink. Additionally, criteria for evaluating whether a discussion is critical include: (a) structures that are in place to ensure inclusivity, (b) time limits, (c) mutual respect, (d) foci on similarities and differences that emerge, (e) a shared power differential, and (f) active listening as the primary goal (Brookfield, 2012).

**Case Studies.**    The case study method incorporates active learning and provides learners with a variety of important skills; more specifically, active learning helps learners develop problem-solving, critical reasoning, and analytical skills, all of which are valuable tools that prepare learners to make better decisions and become better learners (Kunselman & Johnson, 2004; Popil, 2010). Case studies can also provide opportunities for learners to practice critical thinking skills in various leadership scenarios (e.g., Burbach et al., 2004; Powley & Taylor, 2014). To demonstrate this, Jenkins and Cutchens (2010) provided case studies for learners to analyze and apply the "12 actions a leader can take to lead critically" (see Jenkins & Cutchens, 2011; see also Chapter 2) to determine instances in which leaders' decision-making processes excelled or broke down. Additionally, opportunities are provided for learners to make decisions in scenarios where action has not yet been taken.

**Critical Reflection.**    Scholars have alluded to practicing critical reflection—a behavior that integrates personal experiences with new learning and understanding—to engage and mobilize learners to act on new ideas and to challenge conventional thinking in both theory and practice (Jones, Simonetti, & Vielhaber-Hermon, 2000; Reynolds, 1999). By creating opportunities to practice critical leadership, instructors can encourage and facilitate the important connection between critical thinking and leadership development (see also Guthrie & King, 2004; Stedman, 2009). Yet, engaging in critical reflection can create student discomfort and dissonance (Brookfield, 1994; Dewey, 1933; Reynolds, 1999). Nonetheless, as Fink (2013) and others assert, discomfort often means learners are really thinking and consequently really learning. Moreover, when reflection is absent, there is the constant risk of making poor decisions and bad judgments (Brookfield, 1995). For example, without reflection, leaders may be convinced of their invincibility by past successes and fail to consider other viewpoints, with possibly disastrous consequences (Densten & Gray, 2001). Similarly, leaders may avoid reflecting on a course of action because such reflection might challenge their favorable perceptions of themselves (Conger, 1992). In leadership education, deep reflective learning requires learners to consider the underlying dynamics of power and to question basic assumptions and practices. For example, learners could be required to reassess the power they use in leadership situations to achieve their desired results (Jenkins & Cutchens, 2011) through use of counterstorytelling, as discussed in Chapter 4.

## Conclusion

No specific combination of knowledge, pedagogy, praxis, discussion, case study, and critical reflection can ensure integration of critical thinking in leadership education. Further, no secret recipe exists to perfectly evaluate critical leadership outcomes, and there is no concrete standard for measuring how theory is applied to practice. Nonetheless, the logical, educationally grounded, and intentional approach offered here is deeply rooted in student leadership development and leadership education theories and pedagogical approaches, and it presents a process that demonstrates practice to empower and engage our emerging leaders. Further, the process supports a foundation for the creation of leadership-learning contexts capable of developing critical thinking skills and dispositions in undergraduate learners.

The underlying premise of the model demonstrates the need for constant evaluation of the associated processes. Through intentional and focused data collection, analysis, and interpretation, reports can provide valuable insight into the creation of holistic leadership- learning opportunities that prioritize the development of critical thinking. For instructors teaching in leadership programs, their imperative is to build a context to facilitate the process of leadership learning first, utilize critical thinking as a construct within that process, and evaluate learning outcomes. Together, the model bridges experiential leadership education with critical thinking, action, and accountability.

## References

Andenoro, A. C., Allen, S. J., Haber-Curran, P., Jenkins, D. M., Sowcik, M., Dugan, J. P., & Osteen, L. (2013). *National leadership education research agenda 2013–2018: Providing strategic direction for the field of leadership education.* Retrieved from http://leadershipeducators.org/ResearchAgenda

Bailin, S., Case, R., Coombs, J. R., & Daniels, L. B. (1999). Conceptualizing critical thinking. *Journal of Curriculum Studies, 31*(3), 285–302.

Brookfield, S. D. (1994). *Understanding and facilitating adult learning: A comprehensive analysis of principles and effective practices.* San Francisco, CA: Jossey-Bass.

Brookfield, S. D. (1995). What it means to think critically. In J. T. Wren (Ed.), *The leader's companion* (pp. 379–388). New York, NY: The Free Press.

Brookfield, S. D. (2012). *Teaching for critical thinking: Tools and techniques to help learners question their assumptions.* San Francisco, CA: Jossey-Bass.

Burbach, M. E., Matkin, G. S., & Fritz, S. M. (2004). Teaching critical thinking in an introductory leadership course utilizing active learning strategies: A confirmatory study. *College Student Journal, 38*(3), 482–493.

Burke, R. J., & Cooper, C. L. (2004). *Leading in turbulent times: Managing in the new world of work.* Malden, MA: Blackwell.

Conger, J. (1992). *Learning to lead: The art of transforming managers into leaders.* San Francisco, CA: Jossey-Bass.

Conger, J. (2013). Mind the gaps: What limits the impact of leadership education. *Journal of Leadership Studies, 6*(4), 77–83.

Cross, K. P. (2002). *The role of class discussion in the learning-centered classroom* (The Cross Papers No. 6). Phoenix, AZ: League for Innovation in the Community College and Educational Testing Service.

Densten, I. L., & Gray, J. H. (2001). Leadership development & reflection: What is the connection? *The International Journal of Education Management. 15*(3), 119–124.

Dess, G. G., & Picken, J. C. (2000). Changing roles: Leadership in the 21st century. *Organizational Dynamics, 28*(3), 18–33.

Dewey, J. (1933). *How we think: A restatement of the relation of reflective thinking to the educative process.* Boston, MA: Houghton Mifflin.

Ennis, R. H. (1993). Critical thinking assessment. *Theory into Practice, 32*(3), 179–186.

Facione, P. A., & Facione, N. C. (1994). *The California critical thinking dispositions inventory and the National League for Nursing Accreditation requirement in critical thinking* (Resource Paper). Millbrae: California Academic Press.

Fink, L. D. (2013). *Creating significant learning experiences: An integrated approach to designing college courses* (2nd ed.). San Francisco, CA: Jossey-Bass.

Guthrie, V. A., & King, S. N. (2004). Feedback-intensive programs. In C. D. McCauley & E. Van Velsor (Eds.), *The Center for Creative Leadership handbook of leadership development 2* (2nd ed., pp. 25–57). San Francisco, CA: Jossey-Bass.

Halpern, D. F. (1996). *Thinking critically about critical thinking: An exercise book to accompany thought and knowledge: An introduction to critical thinking* (3rd ed.). Mahwah, NJ: Erlbaum.

Halpern, D. F. (2002). *Thought and knowledge: An introduction to critical thinking.* Mahwah, NJ: Erlbaum.

Harvey, M., & Jenkins, D. M. (2014). Knowledge, praxis, and reflection: The three critical elements of effective leadership studies programs. *Journal of Leadership Studies, 7*(4), 76–85.

Heifetz, R., Grashow, A., & Linsky, M. (2009). Leadership in a (permanent) crisis. *Harvard Business Review, 87*(7/8), 62–69.

Hobbs, A., 2010. *Teen summit focuses on education, leadership.* Retrieved from http://www.pnwlocalnews.com/south_king/fwm/lifestyle/81599297.html

Jenkins, D. M. (2012). Exploring signature pedagogies in undergraduate leadership education. *Journal of Leadership Education, 11*(1), 1–27.

Jenkins, D. M. (2013). Exploring instructional strategies in student leadership development programming. *Journal of Leadership Studies, 6*(4), 48–62.

Jenkins, D. M., & Cutchens, A. B. (2010, December). *Leading critically: Applied critical thinking in an undergraduate leadership studies course.* Paper presented at the 2010 Leadership Educators Institute, Tampa, FL.

Jenkins, D. M., & Cutchens, A. B. (2011). Leading critically: A grounded theory of applied critical thinking in leadership studies. *Journal of Leadership Education, 10*(2), 1–21.

Jenkins, D. M., & Dugan, J. P. (2013). Context matters: An interdisciplinary studies interpretation of the national leadership education research agenda. *Journal of Leadership Education, 12*(3), 15–29.

Jones, M. E., Simonetti, J. L., & Vielhaber-Hermon, M. (2000). Building a stronger organization through leadership development at Parke-Davis research. *Industrial and Commercial Training, 32*(2), 44–48.

Kennedy, M., Fisher, M. B., & Ennis, R. H. (1991). Critical thinking: Literature review and needed research. In L. Idol and B. F. Jones (Eds.), *Educational values and cognitive instruction: Implications for reform* (pp. 11–40). Hillsdale, NJ: Erlbaum.

Kunselman, J. C., & Johnson, K. A., (2004). Using the case method to facilitate learning. *College Teaching, 52*(3), 87–92.

Moore, B. N., & Parker, R. (2012). *Critical thinking* (10th ed.). Columbus, OH: McGraw Hill.

Patton, M. Q. (2010). *Developmental evaluation: Applying complexity concepts to enhance innovation and use*. New York, NY: Guilford Press.

Paul, R. W., & Binker, A. J. A. (1990). *Critical thinking: What every person needs to survive in a rapidly changing world*. Rohnert Park, CA: Center for Critical Thinking and Moral Critique, Sonoma State University.

Popil, I. (2010). Promotion of critical thinking by using case studies as teaching method. *Nurse Education Today, 31*(2), 204–207.

Powley, E. H., & Taylor, S. N. (2014). Pedagogical approaches to develop critical thinking and crisis leadership. *Journal of Management Education, 38*(4), 560–585.

Reynolds, M. (1999). Critical reflection and management education: Rehabilitating less hierarchical approaches. *Journal of Management Education, 23*(5), 537–553.

Stedman, N. L. P. (2009). Casting the net of critical thinking: A look into the collegiate leadership classroom. *Journal of Leadership Education, 7*(3), 201–218.

Stedman, N. L., & Andenoro, A. C. (2007). Identification of relationships between emotional intelligence skill and critical thinking disposition in undergraduate leadership learners. *Journal of Leadership Education, 6*(1), 190–208.

Sternberg, R. J. (1985). Teaching CT part I: Are we making critical mistakes? *Phi Delta Kappan, 67*, 194–198.

The University of Southern Maine, Lewiston-Auburn College. (2013). *Employee handbook for faculty and staff*. Retrieved from http://www.usm.maine.edu/sites/default/files/lac/EmployeeHandbook2013.pdf

Yukl, G., & Mahsud, R. (2010). Why flexible and adaptive leadership is essential. *Consulting Psychology Journal: Practice and Research, 62*(2), 81–93.

DANIEL M. JENKINS *is an assistant professor of leadership and organizational studies at the University of Southern Maine, Lewiston-Auburn College.*

ANTHONY C. ANDENORO *is an assistant professor of leadership education within the Department of Agricultural Education and the coordinator of the campus-wide leadership minor at the University of Florida.*

6

*This chapter begins the exploration of what leadership education is through examining the relationship between educational involvement and academic autonomy in the development of socially responsible leaders.*

# Developing Socially Responsible Leaders in Academic Settings

*T. W. Cauthen, III*

"Helping students develop the integrity and strength of character that prepare them for leadership may be one of the most challenging and important goals of higher education" (King, 1997, p. 87). This call to action by psychologist Patricia King responds to the decades of deteriorating leadership capacity and the overarching leadership crisis in American society (Astin, 1996; Ehrlich, 2000; Eisenhower Leadership Group, 1996). College graduates today must address increasingly complex and dynamic social problems. Solving these problems requires adaptive and collaborative approaches that incorporate a multitude of global perspectives with the ultimate goal of positive, sustainable social change (Kezar, Carducci, & Contreras-McGavin, 2006).

Colleges and universities are uniquely poised to address this crisis given the significant role they play in developing the leadership capacity of young adults (Pascarella & Terenzini, 2005). Preparing students for leadership roles in society has been a central purpose and stated goal of college and university mission statements since the beginning of higher education in the United States (Astin & Astin, 2000; Zimmerman-Oster & Burkhardt, 1999; also see Chapter 1). Pascarella and Terenzini (2005) provided research demonstrating that students have the capacity to, and actually do, increase their leadership skills during their time in college. Developing the leadership capacity of college students is a worthwhile endeavor, and institutions of higher education have the opportunity to ensure this is happening both inside and outside of the classroom.

I performed a study of institutional practices that further develop socially responsible leadership in academic-related in- and out-of-class settings (Cauthen, 2012). The study established a relationship between

NEW DIRECTIONS FOR HIGHER EDUCATION, no. 174, Summer 2016 © 2016 Wiley Periodicals, Inc.
Published online in Wiley Online Library (wileyonlinelibrary.com) • DOI: 10.1002/he.20190

academic psychosocial identity development and socially responsible leadership. This chapter discusses the practical ways that these findings can be applied in higher education practice.

## Broadening Socially Responsible Leadership Development Beyond the Co-Curriculum

Socially responsible leadership and the social change model of leadership development (SCM) (Higher Education Research Institute [HERI], 1996) are critical approaches for defining and measuring leadership as a primary outcome of the collegiate experience (Association of American Colleges and Universities, 2007; Astin & Astin, 2000; Dugan & Komives, 2010; National Association of Student Personnel Administrators & American College Personnel Association, 2004; U.S. Department of Education, 2006). Specifically designed for college students, the SCM defines leadership as "a purposeful, collaborative, values-based process that results in positive social change" (Komives, Wagner, & Associates, 2009, p. xii; also see Chapter 4).

The Multi-Institutional Study of Leadership, a national study seeking to assess leadership outcomes, reported that mentoring, campus involvement, formal leadership programs, and engagement in community service matter when developing leadership outcomes in college students (Dugan & Komives, 2007). However, given the assumptions of the model, how might students who never engage in these kinds of collegiate experiences still develop socially responsible leadership? Should those students who are not actively engaged in the co-curriculum not become active and engaged leaders who practice socially responsible leadership in their communities? One can answer this question by considering whether and to what extent students develop leadership capacity through their academic pursuits.

## Deepening Socially Responsible Leadership Through Academic Pursuits

Studies of socially responsible leadership demonstrate that students who are engaged in leadership development programs either in the co-curriculum or in formal leadership education curricular experiences develop stronger measures of socially responsible leadership. However, this research has not looked extensively at how students at large can develop the same outcomes. Psychosocial development (Evans, Forney, Guido, Patton, & Renn, 2010; Pascarella & Terenzini, 2005) is a theoretically grounded construct through which to consider a more broad-based student experience (i.e., outside of co-curricular involvement and formal leadership education curricular experiences). Chickering and Reisser's (1993) theory of psychosocial identity development is a widely used and theoretically tested model (Evans et al.,

2010; Pascarella & Terenzini, 2005) by which to frame this new perspective. Because this theory is concerned with the essential developmental tasks of all young adults ages 17 through 25 (Chickering & Reisser, 1993; Winston, Miller, & Cooper, 1999b), it is inclusive of a majority of undergraduate students, regardless of whether they are involved in activities specifically focused on leadership development. Of particular interest are those developmental tasks associated with the academic experiences of college students. These tasks allow one to not distinguish between involved and uninvolved students, but rather to consider factors associated with the academic experiences that all students must develop in order to be successful at institutions of higher education.

The Student Developmental Task and Lifestyle Assessment (SDTLA) (Winston, Miller, & Cooper, 1999a) is an instrument grounded in the psychosocial identity development work of Chickering and Reisser (1993), and it is a useful tool to provide insight into tasks linked to two of Chickering and Reisser's seven vectors of identity development: (1) moving through autonomy toward interdependence, with an emphasis on academic autonomy, and (2) developing purpose, with a specific focus on educational involvement (Winston et al., 1999a, 1999b). The SDTLA's subtasks of educational involvement and academic autonomy provide a strong grouping of developmental tasks that are directly related to the kinds of experiences and challenges that students face at colleges and universities.

In my study (Cauthen, 2012), I addressed this new perspective by utilizing measures of academically related psychosocial developmental tasks to help explain scores on measures of socially responsible leadership. Doing so broadens the conversation to include experiences that all students have (i.e., academic experiences) and to further the work of socially responsible leadership development with college and university students. Moreover, it explores relationships between these two constructs and offers important perspectives on how one might leverage the academic experience to deepen socially responsible leadership development among undergraduate students.

**Why Educational Involvement Matters.**    Educational involvement is a subtask of the SDTLA's establishing and clarifying purpose task (Winston et al., 1999a) and is grounded in Chickering and Reisser's (1993) vector *developing purpose*. Developing purpose is a key developmental outcome for college and university students. It entails intentional decision making; consideration of and reflection on one's interests, options, goals, and plans; and persistence to achieve one's plans and goals. The broader scope of this vector builds future-focused efforts to define and live according to one's purpose. Specifically in the realm of educational involvement, the higher levels of intentionality that students utilize when determining majors and academic goals contribute to a clarified path beyond college that supports alignment of personal interests, interpersonal and family commitments, and vocational aspirations.

NEW DIRECTIONS FOR HIGHER EDUCATION • DOI: 10.1002/he

Higher levels of educational involvement are correlated with higher capacities for socially responsible leadership in all dimensions—individual, group, and societal—as well as one's total capacity for socially responsible leadership. The individual dimension of socially responsible leadership encourages the development of a deep consciousness of self, an exploration and clarification of values in order to align those values with congruent behaviors, and an investment toward action around concepts that are important to the individual (HERI, 1996). The tasks associated with educational involvement (e.g., selecting a major that aligns with one's interests and intellectual ability) are likely to provide experiential opportunities for students to develop the individual-dimension values of socially responsible leadership more fully.

At the group level, socially responsible leadership focuses on the values of collaboration, common purpose, and controversy with civility (HERI, 1996). These leadership values are deepened by tasks associated with educational involvement, such as building relationships with faculty and staff, engaging in dialogue with faculty on discipline-related topics, and demonstrating active-learning habits.

The societal level of socially responsible leadership is concerned with the value of citizenship; it is measured by the extent to which individuals see themselves as members of a community and feel compelled to make that community better. Students begin to develop this value when they are more engaged in the academic life of the college/university. Students who attend lectures and programs not associated with their academic major or who seek out additional activities not related to course requirements are developing higher levels of educational involvement that, in turn, may produce higher levels of socially responsible leadership within the societal dimension. Educational involvement is also positively correlated with one's total capacity for socially responsible leadership, and it is a statistically significant predictor of the societal dimension of socially responsible leadership. This suggests that participating in all of the activities affiliated with educational involvement deepens value development on all of the dimensional scores and subsequently would suggest a higher total capacity for socially responsible leadership.

Ultimately, educational involvement (Winston et al., 1999a) contributes to establishing and clarifying one's purpose. Developing purpose emphasizes a future focus and integration of one's plans and goals into the scope of a larger purpose for one's life (Chickering & Reisser, 1993). Tasks associated with higher levels of educational involvement require students to consider their vocations and suggest high levels of intentional self-assessment and planning in order to achieve goals and plans that are beyond the scope of the college/university experience. Likewise, the value of citizenship associated with the societal dimension of socially responsible leadership suggests that one is connected to communities and to ideas bigger than oneself. It is future-focused in that it connotes a social and civic responsibility to make a contribution that improves the communities of which we are a part. Essentially, encouraging students to be more educationally involved is likely to deepen their value of citizenship.

**Leveraging Educational Involvement.**   Students who have accomplished the educational involvement subtask "have well-defined educational goals and plans, are knowledgeable about available resources, and are actively involved in the academic life of the college/university" (Winston et al., 1999b, p. 11). According to Winston et al. (1999b), in order to increase developmental gains in the area of educational involvement, faculty and staff should focus on three key areas: (1) academic concentration exploration and selection, (2) faculty interaction and mentorship, and (3) active-learning habit development and campus engagement. Students should be knowledgeable about the various options available for academic major exploration and selection. These resources may come in the form of human resources (e.g., faculty, academic advisors), campus resources (e.g., career centers, major/career fairs, websites), or courses (e.g., freshman seminars, courses developed specifically to assist with major/career exploration). Students should also engage with faculty in a variety of ways. These interactions could be as small as visiting a faculty member during office hours, inviting a dialogue about a research project with which the faculty member is engaged, requesting a recommendation for an article or book in an area of interest, or engaging in more long-term mentorship relationships and collaborative research and writing projects. Last, educators should encourage students to be active participants in their learning experiences and to engage with the campus. Cultivating initiative should be a key area of interest—one in which students are driving their educational experiences and taking advantage of the resources and opportunities available to them on campus.

**Why Academic Autonomy Matters.**   Academic autonomy is a subtask of the SDTLA's developing autonomy task (Winston et al., 1999a) and is grounded in Chickering and Reisser's (1993) vector *moving through autonomy toward interdependence*. Moving through autonomy toward interdependence is a key developmental outcome for college and university students. This developmental construct emphasizes the need for emotional and instrumental independence while simultaneously recognizing the need and value of interdependence. Development along this outcome is characterized by students who do not require high levels of reassurance or approval from others and who demonstrate abilities to be self-directed problem solvers but understand their place within the larger community (Chickering & Reisser, 1993). For academic autonomy, this is demonstrated by the capacity to deal with ambiguity and to self-regulate behavior in ways that allow one to accomplish personal goals and fulfill responsibilities.

There are statistically significant positive relationships between academic autonomy and the individual level of socially responsible leadership. In addition, the correlation between academic autonomy and total capacity for socially responsible leadership is statistically significant. The individual dimension of socially responsible leadership is concerned with the development of an accurate self-concept and a deep level of self-awareness, identification of personal values in order to demonstrate congruent behaviors, and a commitment to invest time and energy in causes important to the individual (HERI, 1996). The tasks associated with academic autonomy (e.g., demonstrating effective study habits, exhibiting honed self-discipline, and displaying behaviors associated with independent learners who practice realistic self-appraisal) are likely to provide experiential opportunities for students to develop the individual- dimension values of socially responsible leadership more fully.

Total capacity for socially responsible leadership is a function of the three dimensional measures and one's ability to adapt to constantly evolving environments. Positive correlation between one's total capacity for socially responsible leadership and academic autonomy would suggest that developing the skills associated with academic autonomy more fully would deepen one's total capacity for socially responsible leadership. Those with high levels of academic autonomy know their strengths and weaknesses, self-regulate their behavior, demonstrate discipline, manage ambiguity, and are self-directed problem solvers. These characteristics not only align well with the values associated with the individual dimension, but are also indicators that a student with high levels of academic autonomy might present more readiness for change and thus have a higher capacity for overall socially responsible leadership.

Academic autonomy also emerged as a statistically significant predictor of the individual dimension of socially responsible leadership. The developmental vector, moving through autonomy toward interdependence (Chickering & Reisser, 1993), is the driving theoretical construct behind academic autonomy (Winston et al., 1999a). It is concerned with the level to which one needs reassurance or approval from others, demonstrates self-directed problem solving, and identifies the interconnectedness of self and others in the larger scope of behaviors. Tasks associated with higher levels of academic autonomy require students to know themselves well enough to determine appropriate and effective study habits, exhibit self-discipline, manage ambiguity, and exhibit ability-consistent levels of academic success. Likewise, the values associated with the individual dimension of socially responsible leadership would expect a high level of self-awareness, a commitment to ongoing self-reflection, an articulation of values and congruent behavior, and an investment in action toward a goal or cause that has meaning. Having higher levels of academic autonomy is a positive predictor of individual dimensions of socially responsible leadership. Essentially, encouraging a student to be more academically autonomous is likely to deepen his or her values associated with the individual dimension of socially responsible leadership (i.e., consciousness of self, congruence, and commitment).

**Leveraging Academic Autonomy.** Students who show high levels of accomplishment in academic autonomy "have the capacity to deal well with ambiguity and to monitor and control their behavior in ways that allow them to attain personal goals and fulfill responsibilities" (Winston et al., 1999b, p. 11). In order to increase developmental gains in the area of academic autonomy, faculty and staff should consider the following areas of focus: (a) academic preparation and performance and (b) self-directed and independent learning. Students should know about resources that assist in the development and honing of effective study habits, as well as tutorial and library assistance. These resources could be offered through a number of venues, such as study skills workshops, library tours and reference seminars, or tutoring centers. Educators should also encourage self-directed and independent learning. Faculty should consider pedagogical techniques, such as problem-based learning, critical pedagogy, or critical thinking, that introduce high levels of ambiguity and self-directed learning. Another example is to reconsider and perhaps avoid the use of faculty-designed rubrics or well-defined and detailed assignments. Instead, allow students to engage in navigating the ambiguity of rubric development and assignment completion in order to increase their levels of independent learning. Utilizing scaffolding techniques in class structure with the use of peer leader co-instructors can also provide opportunities for academic autonomy. For many students, working to accomplish this subtask includes cultivating stronger time-management skills, improving self-discipline, and developing the ability to manage course loads (e.g., juggling multiple course assignments and due dates, maintaining or deepening interests in course/discipline content). Students can enhance these skills by attending time-management workshops, charting deadlines, and developing rewards structures for accomplishing tasks. Students should also utilize their academic advisors to assist with academic course planning.

## Emphasizing Student Development in Conjunction With Student Learning

Educational involvement and academic autonomy do matter when considering how to increase a student's capacity for socially responsible leadership. Educational involvement and academic autonomy are developmental tasks that are most often influenced through the curricular experience; however, there are opportunities for both student affairs and academic affairs educators to bridge the gap in order to ensure that students are experiencing success in these areas and, by extension, to increase students' capacities for socially responsible leadership. Building stronger partnerships between academic affairs and student affairs creates opportunities for this exchange to occur more naturally and intentionally. For example, the College of Family and Consumer Sciences' Student Success and Advising Center at the

University of Georgia utilizes a college-specific unit within the university setting focused on student success, advising, and leadership. This provides an opportunity for student affairs experts to situate themselves within the curricular setting in order to enhance a student development focus within a curricular learning environment. Service learning, study abroad, domestic study trips, internships, discipline-based student organization involvement, and research opportunities are just a few areas in which student affairs staff work with students in this specialized office (for more information, see http://www.fcs.uga.edu/ssac).

## Leveraging Mission-Centered/Mission-Driven Work

There is a connection between academic developmental tasks and the development of socially responsible leadership. Although I have outlined several strategies for leveraging growth in the areas of educational involvement and academic autonomy, it is crucial that the discussion also include the critical role of mission-centered and mission-driven work. As was stated in Chapter 1, many colleges and universities include as a central part of their mission the development of future civic leaders (Astin & Astin, 2000; Zimmerman-Oster & Burkhardt, 1999). Is it not important, then, to ensure that the mission is driving the work at institutions of higher education? I argue that campuses should reframe the context in which this mission-driven work is happening. For example, it is important to encourage faculty to engage with students not only because it assists with student success in the classroom, but also because it may contribute to the larger outcome of developing socially responsible, civic leaders of the future. Creating this shift may be difficult, but advocating for it creates a number of opportunities.

## Emphasizing the Importance of Collaboration

Collaboration may not be a customary approach at some colleges and universities, but in the development of socially responsible leadership, collaboration between different college or university functions is essential.

**Share the Benefits With Faculty.** How can we expect faculty and staff to understand the full scope of work and outcomes if we do not share the information and create structures that support and reward engagement? Educating faculty and staff about the ways in which academic developmental tasks are associated with developing socially responsible leadership is essential. Consider how faculty development centers (e.g., a campus center for teaching and learning) might utilize faculty orientation to share information about how these concepts are related. Moreover, consider how faculty engagement is valued in tenure and promotion procedures. Utilize professional development opportunities to educate academic advisors about their important roles in increasing students' capacities for socially responsible leadership. Further, contemplate how this new context creates new opportunities for student affairs and academic affairs to partner. These partnerships could be through course offerings (e.g., career/major exploration courses) and student success initiatives focused on key developmental tasks such as academic success and preparation (e.g., tutoring services, study skill development, and time management workshops).

**Share the Benefits With Students.** Yet another collaborative opportunity lies in how new students are introduced to the institution. My research, along with that of others (e.g., Komives, Owen, Longerbeam, Mainella, & Osteen, 2005; Owen, 2008), demonstrates that precollege leadership matters. A recent study also suggests that these students are poised for conversations about socially responsible leadership (Cauthen, 2010). These findings suggest that educators should share the benefits of developing strong levels of educational involvement and academic autonomy as just one of perhaps many academic experiences that contribute to the development of socially responsible leadership. New student orientation or freshman seminars may be excellent venues in which student affairs and academic affairs could partner to share and teach, as well as support, students as they begin their academic journeys. This same kind of partnership could, and should, be mirrored beyond the first year. Collaborative approaches to this work ensure that information and resources are being translated across the institution so that students will receive the maximum benefit.

## Conclusion

This chapter introduced a new framework by which we can think about developing socially responsible leadership among all college students, not just those who choose to be involved in the co-curriculum. By taking small but intentional steps, institutions of higher education have the power to fulfill their missions of developing the civic leaders of the future. Leveraging aspects of the curricular learning experience by emphasizing the developmental tasks of educational involvement and academic autonomy can produce significant gains in students' socially responsible leadership capacities.

## References

Association of American Colleges and Universities. (2007). *College learning for the new global century*. Washington, DC: Author.

Astin, A. W., & Astin, H. S. (2000). *Leadership reconsidered: Engaging higher education in social change*. Battle Creek, MI: W. K. Kellogg Foundation.

Astin, H. S. (1996, July/August). Leadership for social change. *About Campus, 1*(3), 4–10.

Cauthen, T. W., III. (2010, August). *Exploring first-year students' understandings and conceptualizations of leadership through a leadership education seminar course* (Unpublished doctoral pilot study). University of Georgia, Athens.

Cauthen, T. W., III. (2012). *Intersections of psychosocial identity development and socially responsible leadership: Developing socially responsible leaders in academic settings* (Unpublished doctoral dissertation). University of Georgia, Athens.

Chickering, A. W., & Reisser, L. (1993). *Education and identity* (2nd ed.). San Francisco, CA: Jossey-Bass.

Dugan, J. P., & Komives, S. R. (2007). *Developing leadership capacity in college students: Findings from a national study* (Report from the Multi-Institutional Study of Leadership). College Park, MD: National Clearinghouse for Leadership Programs.

Dugan, J. P., & Komives, S. R. (2010). Influence on college students' capacities for socially responsible leadership. *Journal of College Student Development, 51*(5), 525–549.

Ehrlich, T. (2000). *Civic responsibility in higher education.* Phoenix, AZ: Oryx Press.

Eisenhower Leadership Group. (1996). *Democracy at risk: How schools can lead.* Washington, DC: U.S. Department of Education.

Evans, N. J., Forney, D. S., Guido, F. M., Patton, L. D., & Renn, K. A. (2010). *Student development in college: Theory, research, and practice* (2nd ed.). San Francisco, CA: Jossey-Bass.

Higher Education Research Institute (HERI). (1996). *A social change model of leadership development: Guidebook version III.* College Park, MD: National Clearinghouse for Leadership Programs.

Kezar, A., Carducci, R., & Contreras-McGavin, M. (2006). Rethinking the "L" word in higher education: The revolution of research on leadership. *ASHE Higher Education Report, 31*(6). San Francisco: Jossey-Bass.

King, P. M. (1997). Character and civic education: What does it take? *Educational Record, 78*(3–4), 87–90.

Komives, S. R., Owen, J. E., Longerbeam, S., Mainella, F. C., & Osteen, L. (2005). Developing a leadership identity: A grounded theory. *Journal of College Student Development, 6,* 593–611.

Komives, S. R., Wagner, W., & Associates. (2009). *Leadership for a better world: Understanding the social change model of leadership development.* San Francisco, CA: Jossey-Bass.

National Association of Student Personnel Administrators & American College Personnel Association. (2004). *Learning reconsidered: A campus-wide focus on the student experience.* Washington, DC: Author.

Owen, J. E. (2008). Towards an empirical typology of collegiate leadership development programs: Examining effects on student self-efficacy and leadership for social change (Unpublished doctoral dissertation). University of Maryland, College Park. Retrieved from ProQuest Dissertations and Theses.

Pascarella, E. T., & Terenzini, P. T. (2005). *How college affects students: A third decade of research.* San Francisco, CA: Jossey-Bass.

U.S. Department of Education. (2006). *A test of leadership: Charting the future of U.S. higher education.* Washington, DC: Author.

Winston, R. B., Jr., Miller, T. K., & Cooper, D. (1999a). *Student developmental task and lifestyle assessment.* Athens, GA: Student Development Associates.

Winston, R. B., Jr., Miller, T. K., & Cooper, D. (1999b). *Student developmental task and lifestyle assessment inventory manual.* Athens, GA: Student Development Associates.

Zimmerman-Oster, K., & Burkhardt, J. C. (1999). *Leadership in the making: Impact and insights from leadership development programs in U.S. colleges and universities.* Battle Creek, MI: W. K. Kellogg Foundation.

*T. W. CAUTHEN III is assistant vice president for academic, campus, and community partnerships in the division of student affairs at the University of Georgia.*

7

*This chapter continues the discussion of what leadership education is and highlights the importance of emotionally intelligent leadership. The authors assert the need for deliberate practice and better collaboration between student affairs, academic affairs, and academic departments to develop emotionally intelligent leaders.*

# Developing Emotionally Intelligent Leadership: The Need for Deliberate Practice and Collaboration Across Disciplines

*Scott J. Allen, Marcy Levy Shankman, Paige Haber-Curran*

The collegiate context is an ideal practice field for leadership development. Not only did we, the authors, gain invaluable experience in campus leadership initiatives, but we also witnessed firsthand students' growth as leaders. The collegiate context is an ideal environment for a number of reasons. First, if leadership is a process of working together with others to influence change, activities such as student organizations and group projects provide positive environments for students to influence others without having formal authority. Second, the collegiate context is generally supportive and growth oriented. Barring gross negligence, student leaders are rarely "fired" and have an opportunity to learn and grow from their successes and failures. Finally, students have access to multiple learning opportunities, whether in the classroom, in co-curricular settings, from mentors, or through peer modeling. In other words, resources associated with growth are often plentiful and available for students.

Given the unique attributes of the higher education context and the types of programming often afforded to students, we suggest that although higher education could provide an optimal practice field for developing emotionally intelligent leadership, *we are not there yet.* The purpose of this chapter is threefold. First, we discuss the importance of emotions in leadership and one specific model, emotionally intelligent leadership (Shankman, Allen, & Haber-Curran, 2015). Second, we highlight how the literature on

NEW DIRECTIONS FOR HIGHER EDUCATION, no. 174, Summer 2016  © 2016 Wiley Periodicals, Inc.
Published online in Wiley Online Library (wileyonlinelibrary.com) • DOI: 10.1002/he.20191

expertise applies to leadership development, and, in particular, we explore how the concepts of the practice field and, more specifically, deliberate practice apply to developing emotionally intelligent leadership. We conclude with a discussion of how collaboration between student affairs, academic affairs, and academic departments can yield more seamless and holistic learning experiences for students. Throughout the chapter, we highlight programs and institutions that we feel are seamless in their approaches to developing leadership (Guthrie & Bovio, 2014).

## Emotion and Leadership

In practice, there is little consistency in the multiple approaches used in the field of leadership education and development. Instructors who teach reading, accounting, biology, chemistry, and mathematics have clear approaches to scaffolding their specific topics, but a clear stepwise approach does not currently exist in leadership education. Although we do not advocate for one singular approach, we do suggest the field of leadership education would benefit from intentional thought and even schools of thought to guide leadership development. Although some textbooks in leadership education (e.g., Northouse, 2012; Yukl, 2012) attempt to do this, there continues to be a need to scaffold appropriate content given the objectives, learner demographics, contexts, and available resources.

One topic we consider foundational for leadership development and worthy of study is emotions and, more specifically, emotional intelligence (EI) (Hogan & Warrenfeltz, 2003; Lord & Hall, 2005). Awareness and regulation of emotions in self and others is a critical skill of any leader (Goleman, 2000). One simply needs to look at the critical activities of leadership to understand why emotions are so important. First, effective leadership often involves engaging others in a cause. This activity, by nature, is an emotional process. In addition, leadership involves helping others navigate ill-structured or ill-defined problems, which is emotionally taxing work for both the group and for the leader, who may hold ultimate responsibility (perhaps self-imposed) for the success or failure of the group. These types of problems often include a prolonged period of uncertainty and confusion as the group works to determine a direction or course of action. Throughout the process of establishing vision or direction, leadership also involves navigating difficult conversations, conflict, and personal agendas and, in many cases, balancing the needs of competing factions. These responsibilities cause stress and, of course, emotional reactions in self and others.

*How* individuals and groups move through these natural challenges can inspire action or deenergize them and cause additional conflict. We assert that setting a positive emotional tone is a necessary aspect of leadership; we also recognize that contextual difference may necessitate other emotional tones or adaptive responses. However, generally speaking, we are confident

NEW DIRECTIONS FOR HIGHER EDUCATION • DOI: 10.1002/he

that setting a positive emotional tone is a crucial capacity within a leadership process.

There are two primary streams of research on emotional intelligence, the ability model and mixed models, and although they have similarities (e.g., awareness of emotions in self and others), there are fundamental differences between them. For instance, the ability model of EI (Salovey & Mayer, 1990) views EI as an intelligence and consists of four hierarchical branches that suggest some EI abilities are more psychologically complex than others. A second approach, the mixed model approach, is widespread in corporate practice but has been challenged by many in academic circles for blending emotional intelligence with social intelligence or leadership (Antonakis, Ashkanasy, & Dasborough, 2009). There are three primary models in this group: trait emotional intelligence (Mavroveli, Petrides, Rieffe, & Bakker, 2007), the performance model of EI (Goleman, 1995), and Bar-On's (2010) model. Although Bar-On and Goleman initially suggested their models were about emotional intelligence, they now use *emotional-social intelligence,* perhaps in response to critiques of the mixed model approach.

Regardless of one's preferred model (see Allen, Shankman, & Miguel, 2012, for a more in-depth discussion), emotional intelligence is about being aware of one's emotions and emotions in others and being able to regulate them. In our own work, we identify these capacities as emotional self-perception, emotional self-control, displaying empathy, and inspiring others (Shankman et al., 2015). The first two capacities, emotional self-perception and emotional self-control, are inwardly focused, and the next two capacities, displaying empathy and inspiring others, occur when engaging with others (see Table 7.1).

A campus-based example of students learning about their emotions in the context of leadership occurs at Christopher Newport University. Kate Sheridan, associate director of the President's Leadership Program, shared that students have continuous opportunities to explore "how their emotions relate to and influence both their leadership and where their sense of purpose lies" (personal communication, May 29, 2014). One example of when this occurs is during the first-year orientation program when students participate in a session on vulnerability and its connection to leadership and collaboration. In general, as students progress through the program, they have opportunities to further explore this idea through workshops, student organizations, and one-on-one meetings with staff.

## Emotionally Intelligent Leadership

Our model of emotionally intelligent leadership (EIL) encompasses three facets: consciousness of self, consciousness of others, and consciousness of context. Across the three EIL facets are 19 capacities that equip individuals

**Table 7.1. Emotional Self-Perception, Emotional Self-Control, Displaying Empathy, and Inspiring Others**

| | |
|---|---|
| Emotional Self-Perception | Identifying emotions and their impact on behavior. Emotional self-perception is about describing, naming, and understanding your emotions. Emotionally intelligent leaders are aware of how situations influence emotions and how emotions impact interactions with others. |
| Emotional Self-Control | Consciously moderating emotions. Emotional self-control means intentionally managing your emotions and understanding how and when to demonstrate them appropriately. Emotionally intelligent leaders take responsibility for regulating their emotions and are not victims of them. |
| Displaying Empathy | Being emotionally in tune with others. Empathy is about perceiving and addressing the emotions of others. Emotionally intelligent leaders place a high value on the feelings of others and respond to their emotional cues. |
| Inspiring Others | Energizing individuals and groups. Inspiration occurs when people are excited about a better future. Emotionally intelligent leaders foster feelings of enthusiasm and commitment to organizational mission, vision, and goals. |

*Source: Emotionally Intelligent Leadership: A Guide for College Students* (2nd ed.), by M. L. Shankman, S. J. Allen, and P. Haber-Curran, 2015, San Francisco, CA: Jossey-Bass.

with the knowledge, skills, perspectives, and attitudes needed to achieve desired outcomes (Shankman et al., 2015).

We define the three facets as follows:

1. Consciousness of self: Demonstrating emotionally intelligent leadership involves awareness of personal abilities, emotions, and perceptions. Consciousness of self is about prioritizing the inner work of reflection and introspection and appreciating that self-awareness is a continual and ongoing process.
2. Consciousness of others: Demonstrating emotionally intelligent leadership involves awareness of the abilities, emotions, and perceptions of others. Consciousness of others is about intentionally working with and influencing individuals and groups to affect positive change.
3. Consciousness of context: Demonstrating emotionally intelligent leadership involves awareness of the setting and situation. Consciousness of context is about paying attention to how environmental factors and internal group dynamics affect the process of leadership. (Shankman et al., 2015)

When discussing the three facets, we use the metaphor of signal strength (see Figure 7.1). In the context of Wi-Fi networking, the signal strength determines one's ability to connect. In the metaphor, we place the individual at the center (the dot) and each subsequent bar is one of the three facets: consciousness of self, consciousness of others, or

**Figure 7.1.  Signal Strength**

consciousness of context. One bar of signal strength will work, but there is often static and noise, and things may move slowly. Additional bars indicate a better connection and result in better performance. We suggest that, generally speaking, working with all three bars at full strength will allow an individual to more effectively connect with and engage others.

In addition to the three facets, there are 19 capacities of EIL. The *American Heritage Dictionary* defines *capacity* as "ability to perform or produce; capability" (n.d.). The 19 capacities (Table 7.2) bring life to the three facets of EIL and are both learnable and teachable. Likewise, we have included 4 capacities that most closely align with emotional intelligence (emotional self-perception, emotional self-control, displaying empathy,

**Table 7.2.  The 19 Capacities of Emotionally Intelligent Leadership**

**Consciousness of Self**
Emotional self-perception: Identifying emotions and their impact on behavior
Emotional self-control: Consciously moderating emotions
Authenticity: Being transparent and trustworthy
Healthy self-esteem: Having a balanced sense of self
Flexibility: Being open and adaptive to change
Optimism: Having a positive outlook
Initiative: Taking action
Achievement: Striving for excellence

**Consciousness of Others**
Displaying empathy: Being emotionally in tune with others
Inspiring others: Energizing individuals and groups
Coaching others: Enhancing the skills and abilities of others
Capitalizing on difference: Benefiting from multiple perspectives
Developing relationships: Building a network of trusting relationships
Building teams: Working with others to accomplish a shared purpose
Demonstrating citizenship: Fulfilling responsibilities to the group
Managing conflict: Identifying and resolving conflict
Facilitating change: Working toward new directions

**Consciousness of Context**
Analyzing the group: Interpreting group dynamics
Assessing the environment: Interpreting external forces and trends

*Source: Emotionally Intelligent Leadership: A Guide for College Students* (2nd ed.), by M. L. Shankman, S. J. Allen, and P. Haber-Curran, 2015, San Francisco, CA: Jossey-Bass.

inspiring others) and 15 other capacities that are closely aligned with effective leadership. While we do not assert that these are the *only* capacities of effective leadership, we believe they serve as positive starting points for student leaders.

Emotionally intelligent leadership provides a helpful framework and perspective for student leaders wishing to develop their leadership abilities. Not only is the EIL model designed with students in mind, but it also integrates several important concepts into one. First, the model addresses the complexity of any leadership challenge and emphasizes the need to focus on self, others, and context. In addition, the model places an emphasis on emotions and their role in leadership. Finally, the model is situated in the context of the target learners—students in high school, college, and graduate school. By doing so, we meet students where they are and provide examples that resonate and connect with them.

## Developing Emotionally Intelligent Leaders: Lessons From the Literature on Expertise

To this point, we have established the importance of emotions as an essential topic in leadership and have shared one approach, emotionally intelligent leadership. In this section, we explore how the expertise literature can help program architects develop a curriculum that will develop emotionally intelligent leadership.

In the context of secondary and higher education, students have access to different types of learning opportunities—cognitive, humanistic, and behavioral (Merriam & Caffarella, 1999). Learning that focuses primarily on theory and the mental processes associated with leadership are primarily cognitive in nature. These types of experiences often occur in the academic classroom. Humanistic programming focuses on topics such as motivations, emotion, values, identity, and personal growth—in essence, the inner work of a leader. These experiences take place in the classroom at times, but are more often present in co-curricular programming associated with student affairs. A behavioral approach focuses on skill development, such as public speaking, managing conflict, running meetings, motivating others, and decision making. Although some learning interventions incorporate behaviorism via role-play and simulation, there is often not enough time, attention, and focus given to behavioral development in both the academic and student affairs realms to facilitate mastery or expertise. We assert that the paucity of behavioral learning interventions is the Achilles' heel of leadership development.

A valuable resource to address this concern lies in the expertise literature, which is a valuable resource for developing emotionally intelligent leaders in and out of the classroom. Interestingly, the "born versus made" debate that occurs in the leadership literature also happens in the expertise literature. Fortunately, there is a similar conclusion; Ericsson, Prietula, and Cokely (2007) suggest "experts are always made, not born" (p. 116).

Glaser and Chi (1998) provide several conclusions about expertise. First, experts rarely achieve a similar status in multiple domains (medical expertise does not equal expertise in law). Second, experts see large and meaningful patterns that novices simply cannot see. For instance, a physician looks at the composite results and patterns of a complete blood count, whereas novices only see the discrete results for each individual result. A third distinction is that experts can generally do their work quickly. What may take the novice hours will take the expert minutes or even seconds. This occurs for two primary reasons: practice and the ability to quickly see patterns in the environment or activity (Glaser & Chi, 1998). A fourth distinction has to do with memory. Studies suggest experts have better short- and long-term memories. In fact, the automaticity of certain functions frees up space for additional knowledge. The ability to look at a problem from a deeper level also distinguishes experts from novices. In other words, "both experts and novices have conceptual categories, but ... the experts' categories are semantically or principle-based, whereas the categories of the novices are syntactically or surface-feature oriented" (Glaser & Chi, 1998, p. xix). A sixth difference is the amount of time spent defining a problem. Experts spend more time analyzing a problem before beginning to solve the task. In fact, experts think more critically and identify constraints in the problem-solving process. Finally, experts have superior self-monitoring skills. Experts are more aware of their limitations and are more likely to know when they have made a mistake. Although this is not an exhaustive list of ideal attributes, we argue that these would serve leaders well. Individuals with a great deal of knowledge about leadership, the ability to diagnose challenges, and superior planning and meta-monitoring abilities have the attributes of a leader.

## The Role of Deliberate Practice in Developing Emotionally Intelligent Leaders

The concept of a practice field is an essential component of developing emotionally intelligent leadership. While this practice field exists in other domains, such as mathematics, debate, public speaking, spelling, and athletics, it is essentially nonexistent in the realm of leadership development. And although sources of learning such as service-learning (see Chapter 2), problem-based learning (see Chapter 3), and simulations may provide short-term opportunities, we struggle to identify any long-term and sustained environments that provide opportunities for individuals to engage in ongoing and consistent deliberate practice similar to other domains such as athletics, music, and debate. Many discuss the necessity of experience (e.g., McCall, 2010), yet *experience* does not necessarily mean one is engaged in deliberate practice and is truly gaining expertise (Day, 2010; DeRue & Ashford, 2010).

Although it is unlikely that "expert" leaders can be fully developed in the context of a collegiate experience, we can provide learning experiences that better create the conditions for doing so. This will require coordination, collaboration, and the introduction of deliberate practice. Deliberate practice involves intentionally working on developing oneself through continuous, focused, and ongoing effort and attention. There are several attributes of deliberate practice that program architects should consider. First, there is a focus on what one currently *cannot do,* repetition, and incremental improvement. Outside of one-time simulations and service-learning opportunities, current collegiate programming rarely affords an individual opportunities for repetition until mastery has occurred. Second, there is the need for immediate feedback, as development of expertise requires coaches who are capable of giving constructive, even painful, feedback. Real experts are extremely motivated students who seek out such feedback. They are also skilled at understanding when and if a coach's advice doesn't work for them (Ericsson et al., 2007). Currently, a great deal of time is spent *talking* about leadership in classrooms and workshops, and little time is dedicated to *practicing* leadership or providing real-time feedback to students. Most leadership occurs in environments where students will not receive real-time constructive feedback (e.g., Greek organization, programming board).

Third, there is a sustained commitment of time over a period of years (Bloom, 1985; Ericsson, Krampe, & Tesch-Römer, 1993). In fact, "the amount of time an individual is engaged in deliberate practice is monotonically related to that individual's acquired performance" (Ericsson et al., 1993, p. 368). Although students may spend a great deal of time in leadership roles over the course of their college careers, they may not be engaged in sustained leadership activities; thus, important learning opportunities are missed. Fourth, deliberate practice is different from work and play. As Ericsson et al. (1993) stated, "deliberate practice is a highly structured activity, the explicit goal of which is to improve performance. Specific tasks are invented to overcome weakness, and performance is carefully monitored to provide cues for way to improve it further" (p. 368). Rarely are individual development plans created for students to improve upon weaknesses, and, as a result, the process is haphazard and opportunities are missed for intentional development. Infrequently we see examples such as problem-based learning referenced in Chapter 3, in which students are actively involved in deep learning through intentional development.

Finally, the acquisition of expertise requires access to resources such as time, educators, facilities, materials, and money. Expert performers have often "overcome a number of constraints [and] obtained early access to instructors, maintained high levels of deliberate practice throughout development, received continued parental and environmental support, and avoided disease and injury" (Ericsson et al., 1993, p. 400).

NEW DIRECTIONS FOR HIGHER EDUCATION • DOI: 10.1002/he

The Imprint Leadership Program at the University of Illinois demonstrates one approach to deliberate practice as it pertains to student leadership development. The program focuses on coaching and feedback for the students (for more information, see http://www.illinoisleadership .illinois.edu/programs/imprint.asp). Alumni serve as coaches, and these alumni are assigned to students with whom they share common academic and professional interests. Coaches help their students work toward the students' identified goals, serve as small-group facilitators for the program, and operate within a framework of perpetual learning and succeeding as a person of influence in new environments. If we were to overlay EIL onto Imprint Leadership, we would see how the students demonstrate consciousness of self (e.g., identifying goals, understanding individual strengths and limitations) and consciousness of context (e.g., what's needed to achieve given a certain set of conditions, challenges, and opportunities faced as a first-year student or as a new graduate) as they work with their coaches.

## Opportunities for Integration to Develop Emotionally Intelligent Leaders

To this point we have explored emotionally intelligent leadership and a need for a well-balanced approach to leadership development that incorporates the cognitive, humanistic, and behavioral dimensions. We assert that current programming often incorporates the cognitive and humanistic dimensions, while the behavioral dimension is often underdeveloped (e.g., lacks opportunities for deliberate practice). As a result, learning in this realm is lacking. One approach to building a more holistic and seamless experience for students requires integration and cooperation between student affairs, academic affairs, and academic departments. In our experience, academic affairs often excels in the cognitive realm and student affairs often focuses more heavily on the humanistic realm. In essence, we assert that the resources, skill sets, and areas of expertise needed to develop leaders lie in multiple areas of the institution.

Kezar, Hirsch, and Burack (2002), in a publication titled *Understanding the Role of Academic and Student Affairs Collaboration in Creating a Successful Learning Environment,* outlined and described models of collaboration intentionally designed to help develop successful student leaders. Yet, here we are, years later, still exploring the topic. Those outside of higher education may wonder why this is the case, but those of us on the college or university campus know the difficulties and challenges of creating true collaborations. One way to look at the recalcitrance of our institutions and campuses to demonstrate collaboration across units and divisions is to hone in on the difficulties of collaboration. This word is laden with high expectations, false realities, and sincere challenges. Rather than creating a dichotomy of either a successful or unsuccessful collaboration, we recommend appreciating collaboration as a spectrum of choices to be constantly made and assessed around alignment and integration. Three institutions that successfully meet the challenge of collaboration are Florida State University, Elon University, and Christopher Newport University.

Florida State University offers a prime example of integration and cooperation between student affairs and academic affairs. Faculty from the College of Education work with and collaborate with staff from the Center for Leadership and Social Change (L. Osteen, personal communication, May 28, 2014; for more information, see http://thecenter.fsu.edu). Not only is there a faculty line for leadership and social change in the college, but there are also certificate courses and practicums offered that integrate academic coursework with applied learning and reflection. This results in seamless learning that "exists when students are able to engage both within and outside of the classroom experiences that contribute to overall engagement, growth, and learning" (Guthrie & Bovio, 2014, p. 26). Students develop leadership plans and work with staff of the center and with faculty to achieve their goals. They receive feedback and coaching and are then asked to apply what they have learned. For example, students in the Undergraduate Certificate of Leadership Studies program have to complete a leadership experience. Some students complete their experience through an 8-month program in which they may be selected for a student coordinator role. Student coordinators go on to deliver leadership development experiences for other students on campus. The design of the program, in which students learn about leadership, receive feedback through coaching, and practice what they have learned in formal leadership roles, is an applied demonstration of deliberate practice being instituted into a leadership development program.

Elon University integrates EIL into both the classroom and the co-curricular learning environment. The psychology of leadership course incorporates EIL as a model that the students learn in the context of effective leadership. In co-curricular leadership programs, elements of EIL are incorporated when applicable in the coaching that students receive as part of the Leadership Education and Development Program and as part of the Leadership Fellows experience (for more information, see http://www.elon.edu/e-web/students/leadership/LEAD.xhtml). Likewise, The Isabella Cannon Leadership Fellows Program is housed within Elon's Division of Student Life, yet academic faculty are integral to the success of the program (for more information, see http://www.elon.edu/eweb/admissions/Fellows/leadership.xhtml). This program is a 4-year, cohort-based leadership development initiative that incorporates both curricular and co-curricular components (S. Mencarini, personal communication, May 26, 2014). The Fellows coordinate and run three day-long leadership development programs for participants and serve as mentors for successful projects. Throughout their preparation, the fellows are asked to reflect on the role that emotions play in their leadership and their abilities to demonstrate initiative, authenticity, and environmental awareness (three EIL capacities).

NEW DIRECTIONS FOR HIGHER EDUCATION • DOI: 10.1002/he

Elon also has a living-learning community, a leadership advisory board, and faculty fellows; all of these efforts engage students and faculty in intentional efforts to increase the knowledge, skills, and awareness of students in a leadership context.

A final example of cross-divisional collaboration in leadership development efforts is the President's Leadership Program at Christopher Newport University, which spans the curriculum and co-curriculum (for more information, see http://cnu.edu/presidentsleadership/). Students "complete a minor in leadership studies while participating in personal and leadership development opportunities, serving in the local community, getting involved on campus, and upholding rigorous academic standards regardless of their field of study" (K. Sheridan, personal communication, May 23, 2014). Study-abroad options and participation in the International Leadership Association are encouraged as other ways to further academic learning.

## Conclusion

Leadership educators have a unique opportunity to facilitate meaningful student learning. Institutional goals around student leadership development do not fall to either academic or student affairs. All educators have a responsibility, regardless of where they are housed in the institutional structure, to be committed to learning goals related to student leadership development. Recognizing that learning goals for student leadership development are multifaceted, we advocate for a sincere focus on the role that emotions play in leadership. We hope our discussion on the role of emotions in leadership and the presentation of our model of emotionally intelligent leadership provides a useful framework for students' leadership development.

Likewise, we encourage readers to consider ways in which the natural settings of institutions can be designed and promoted as effective practice fields for developing emotionally intelligent leadership. We also hope readers will consider not only the *breadth* of leadership education provided, but also the *depth* of this education, such as learning opportunities that develop capacities in a way that allows for ongoing and deliberate practice. The institutions we highlighted in this chapter are good examples of programs that we feel are moving in the right direction. Holistic, integrative, and seamless approaches to leadership education with a focus on emotionally intelligent leadership can help provide a context from which many of the ideas we have presented in this chapter can become actualized.

## References

Allen, S. J., Shankman, M. L., & Miguel, R. (2012). Emotionally intelligent leadership: An integrative, process-oriented theory of student leadership. *Journal of Leadership Education, 11*(1), 177–203.

Antonakis, J., Ashkanasy, N. M., & Dasborough, M. T. (2009). Does leadership need emotional intelligence? *The Leadership Quarterly, 20*(2), 247–261.

Bar-On, R. (2010). *A broad definition of emotional-social intelligence according to the Bar-On model.* Retrieved from http://www.reuvenbaron.org/wp/the-bar-on-model/

Bloom, B. S. (1985). *Developing talent in young people.* New York, NY: Ballentine Books.

Capacity. (n.d.). In *The American heritage dictionary online.* Retrieved from https://ahdictionary.com/word/search.html?q=capacity

Day, D. V. (2010). The difficulties of learning from experience and the need for deliberate practice. *Industrial and Organizational Psychology, 3*(1), 41–44.

DeRue, S., & Ashford, S. (2010). Power to the people: Where has personal agency gone in leadership development? *Industrial and Organizational Psychology, 3*(1), 24–27.

Ericsson, K. A., Krampe, R. Th., & Tesch-Römer, C. (1993). The role of deliberate practice in the acquisition of expert performance. *Psychological Review, 100*(3), 363–406.

Ericsson, K. A., Prietula, M. J., & Cokely, E. T. (2007). The making of an expert- response. *Harvard Business Review, 85,* 146–147.

Glaser, R., & Chi, M. T. H. (1998). Overview. In R. Glaser, M. T. H. Chi, & M. J. Farr (Eds.), *The nature of expertise* (pp. 15–27). Hillsdale, NJ: Erlbaum.

Goleman, D. (1995). *Working with emotional intelligence.* New York, NY: Bantam Books.

Goleman, D. (2000, March/April). Leadership that gets results. *Harvard Business Review,* March–April, 78–90.

Guthrie, K. L., & Bovio, B. (2014). Undergraduate certificate in leadership studies: An opportunity for seamless learning. *Journal of College and Character, 15*(1), 25–32.

Hogan, R., & Warrenfeltz, R. (2003). Educating the modern manager. *Academy of Management Learning and Education, 2*(1), 74–84.

Kezar, A. J., Hirsch, D., & Burack, C. (2002). *Understanding the role of academic and student affairs collaboration in creating a successful learning environment.* San Francisco, CA: Jossey-Bass.

Lord, R. G., & Hall, R. J. (2005). Identity, deep structure and the development of leadership skill. *The Leadership Quarterly, 16*(4), 591–615.

Mavroveli, S., Petrides, K. V., Rieffe, C., & Bakker, F. (2007). Trait emotional intelligence, psychological well-being and peer-rated social competence in adolescence. *British Journal of Developmental Psychology, 25*(2), 263–275.

McCall, M. W. (2010). Recasting leadership development. *Industrial and Organizational Psychology, 3*(1), 3–19.

Merriam, S. B., & Caffarella, R. S. (1999). *Learning in adulthood: A comprehensive guide* (2nd ed.). San Francisco, CA: Jossey-Bass.

Northouse, P. G. (2012). *Leadership: Theory and practice* (6th ed.). Thousand Oaks, CA: Sage.

Salovey, P., & Mayer, J. D. (1990). Emotional intelligence. *Imagination, Cognition, and Personality, 9*(3), 185–211.

Shankman, M. L., Allen, S. J., & Haber-Curran, P. (2015). *Emotionally intelligent leadership: A guide for college students* (2nd ed.). San Francisco, CA: Jossey-Bass.

Yukl, G. A. (2012). *Leadership in organizations* (8th ed.). Upper Saddle River, NJ: Prentice Hall.

SCOTT J. ALLEN is an associate professor of management at John Carroll University.

MARCY LEVY SHANKMAN is director of Leadership Cleveland and Strategic Initiatives at the Cleveland Leadership Center and principal of MLS Consulting, LLC.

PAIGE HABER-CURRAN is an assistant professor and program coordinator for the Student Affairs in Higher Education program at Texas State University.

NEW DIRECTIONS FOR HIGHER EDUCATION • DOI: 10.1002/he

8

*Moving from why, how, and what, this chapter closes with a focus on how we know the outcomes of leadership education. This final chapter provides an overview of leadership competency development as a critical component of higher education.*

# Leadership Competency Development: A Higher Education Responsibility

*Corey Seemiller*

Competencies are "the core elements in a periodic table of human behavior" (Russ-Eft, 1995, p. 329). However, the definition of *competencies* has been riddled with contradiction, confusion, and lack of consistency. In the 1970s, Spady (1977) referred to the competency movement as "a bandwagon in search of a definition" (p. 9). Not much has changed today, as the definition of competencies ranges from "the collection of knowledge, skills and attitudes" (Mulder, Gulikers, Wesselink, & Biemans, 2008, p. 8) to abilities, motives, traits, and self-concept that result in effective or superior performance (Klein, 1997). The multitude of definitions can be categorized into two main themes: (1) specific knowledge and skills required to perform a particular task or role, and (2) the ability to "carry out valued activities effectively," which constitutes mastery of a general set of high-level competencies (Klein, 1997, p. 3). Defillippi and Arthur (2006) indicate three types of competencies: (1) know-why competencies focus on "career motivation, personal meaning, and identification" (p. 308), (2) know-how competencies reflect specific knowledge and skills related to the job, and (3) know-whom competencies focus on career networks and interpersonal relations. In some definitions of competencies, there is a focus solely on behavior or performance, whereas in others, elements such as attitude are included. In addition, some definitions are limited to learned behavior, whereas others include inherent traits.

Despite the lack of a common definition for competencies, there are some components that appear to be agreed upon. First, competencies should be identified for each task or role in an effort to lay out criteria that will provide direction for an individual to improve his or her capacity. Second, competencies should be measurable. This may entail levels of

New Directions for Higher Education, no. 174, Summer 2016 © 2016 Wiley Periodicals, Inc.
Published online in Wiley Online Library (wileyonlinelibrary.com) • DOI: 10.1002/he.20192

competency acquisition or criteria for competency mastery outlined in a rubric or evaluation. For the purposes of this chapter, *competencies* will be defined as knowledge, values, abilities (skills or motivations), and behaviors that contribute to one's effectiveness in a role or task (Seemiller, 2013).

## The Competency Movement

The concept of competencies has been around since the 1960s. McClelland (1973) is often credited with spurring the development of the competency movement by focusing on the value of competency testing rather than intelligence testing in predicting job success. In the 1980s, the American Management Association conducted a major study on competencies through assessing characteristics associated with effective job performance (Boyatzis, 1982). The 1990s saw a growth of the use of competencies in professional settings as organizations aimed to define values and direction in a time of great change (Garman & Johnson, 2006).

Although Spady (1977) believed that competencies were "rapidly transforming into a bandwagon that promises to be the Great American Educational Fad of the 1970s" (p. 9), the use of competencies is still common today. Organizations from various fields such as nursing (Weston et al., 2008) and the military (Costin, 2009) still use competencies. Even the U.S. Department of Labor's (2014) CareerOneStop offers a searchable database of competency models, or lists of competencies, associated with a multitude of career fields.

There are many uses for competencies in organizations. First, organizations can administer assessments based on an identified set of competencies related to job effectiveness to predict the performance of job candidates or employees (Bartram, 2005). Second, individuals can be trained based on the competencies they need for effectiveness in their jobs (Ennis, 2008). Third, organizations can use competencies to effectively evaluate employees using set criteria and observable behavior (Posthuma & Campion, 2008). Fourth, organizations can create a system for equitable promotion based on competency acquisition or demonstration (Morgeson, Campion, & Levashina, 2009). Finally, organizations can provide compensation that reflects employee competency levels and specific performance (Lawler, 1994).

## Competencies in Higher Education

Competencies are not just integrated into the occupational sector; they also play a role in higher education. There is a great deal of literature on competency-based learning that spans the last 40 years and continues to spur the conversation about higher education's use of competencies as learning tools and forms of measurement. The use of competencies in higher education lies in two distinct approaches. The first is awarding the credit hour for competency demonstration rather than "seat time"

(Klein-Collins, Ikenberry, & Kuh, 2014). This approach can culminate in awarding a degree to a learner who did not participate in a traditional credit-bearing course.

The second uses a more traditional approach by integrating competencies into lesson plans in credit-bearing courses and then assessing student learning and development of those competencies at the conclusion of the course (Klein-Collins et al., 2014). This chapter will address the second aspect of competency use in higher education by focusing on how to identify and integrate competencies into the existing higher education framework through both the curriculum and co-curriculum.

## Overview of Leadership Competencies

Leadership development research for more than the last decade has focused on the identification of leadership competencies for individuals (Spendlove, 2007). Leadership itself as a competency is quite broad, yet many other competencies may be able to contribute to successful leadership, including effective communication, strategic visioning, and critical evaluation. Leadership competency models do not aim to be prescriptive in terms what it takes to be an effective leader; rather, they "attempt to capture the experience, lessons learned, and knowledge of seasoned leaders to provide a guiding framework for the benefit of others and the organization" (Spendlove, 2007, p. 409). Using an overarching framework of leadership competencies provides a "common denominator for leader development ... [that is] portable across: time, levels of authority, levels of responsibility, and unforeseen situations" (Horey, Fallesen, Morath, Cronin, & Cassella, 2004, p. 2).

For more than 100 years, higher education in the United States has been subject to a process of review for quality assurance referred to as *accreditation* (Eaton, 2011). Entire institutions as well as individual academic programs can participate in the accreditation process. Without accreditation, institutions and academic programs can lose their recruitment power, funding streams, and legitimacy, impacting their ability to operate. Accreditation and reaccreditation are awarded to institutions and academic programs that can demonstrate meeting a variety of structural and learning objectives. For academic program accreditation, programs must demonstrate that the curriculum meets the learning outcomes listed in the accrediting manual. For instance, with regard to leadership, how prominent are leadership competencies among the required learning outcomes across various academic programs? Hence, to what extent is leadership truly cross-disciplinary? Chapter 2 begins this discussion by addressing the importance of combined leadership and liberal arts competencies. But do campuses take this cross-disciplinary approach?

**Study Overview.**    In 2008, in an effort to develop a universal leadership competency model for use with students in higher education, I, along with a colleague, Tom Murray, engaged in a robust study using document analysis of seminal documents in student affairs literature and contemporary leadership models (Seemiller & Murray, 2013). The study began as a synthesis of leadership competencies that appeared as standards, outcomes, or components in the Council for the Advancement of Standards in Higher Education (2008) standards, the 2004 American College Personnel Association/National Association of Student Personnel Administrators document *Learning Reconsidered*, the relational leadership model (Komives, Lucas, & McMahon, 1998), the social change model of leadership development (Higher Education Research Institute, 1996), and the five practices of exemplary leadership (Kouzes & Posner, 1995). This document analysis allowed us to probe the texts for leadership competencies and create a master list. This list later became the student leadership competencies model.

After this initial process, we began the analysis of learning outcomes from accredited academic programs to uncover any leadership competencies embedded in those outcomes. We added any competencies not already included in the student leadership competencies model. Between 2009 and 2011, we then analyzed learning outcomes in 475 academic programs from 93 academic accrediting organizations affiliated with the Council for Higher Education Accreditation, the U.S. Department of Education, and the Association of Specialized and Professional Accreditors. Academic programs comprised a variety of degree levels from vocational diplomas to postdoctorate certificates. Through this time period, we made various changes to the initial student leadership competencies model. These included adding emergent competencies, removing immeasurable competencies, and consolidating similar competencies. This reworking of the student leadership competencies model also included classifying competencies into four dimensions: knowledge, value, ability, and behavior (Seemiller, 2013).

In 2013, I undertook the process again because some accredited programs and organizations were no longer in existence, others had been added, and some had simply changed their outcomes. All 522 academic programs from all 97 accrediting organizations included in the Council for Higher Education Accreditation, the U.S. Department of Education, and the Association of Specialized and Professional Accreditors were analyzed using the student leadership competencies model, resulting in the analysis of nearly 18,000 learning outcomes. Changes were made to the student leadership competencies model to reflect the new data, and the final model included 60 competencies, each with four dimensions.

As seen in Figure 8.1, the student leadership competencies model includes eight categories in which the 60 competencies fall. Definitions of the 60 competencies and their dimensions can be found in *The Student Leadership Competencies Guidebook* (Seemiller, 2013).

**Results.**    Results of the study indicate that leadership competencies are present across a variety of academic programs. First, 100% of all 97 accrediting organizations, including the American Bar Association, American

## Figure 8.1.  Student Leadership Competencies

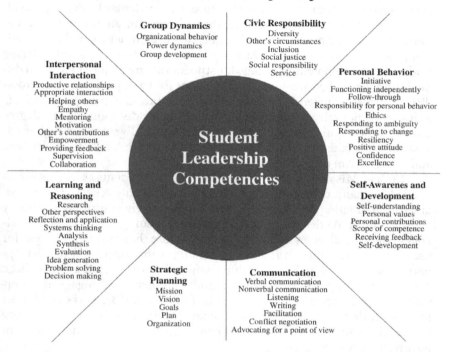

Source: *The Student Leadership Competencies Guidebook,* by C. Seemiller, 2013, San Francisco, CA: Jossey-Bass.

Association of School Librarians, Association to Advance Collegiate Schools of Business, National Association of Schools of Arts and Design, National Association for the Education of Young Children, and Commission on Collegiate Nursing Education, require students to have developed least one leadership competency upon graduation. In addition, the 2013 data indicate that 41% of all accrediting organizations require "leadership" itself as a competency, up from 36.6% in 2008 (Seemiller & Murray, 2013, p. 41). Thirty percent of all accrediting organizations had at least half of their entire set of learning outcomes inclusive of a leadership competency. And of the entire 17,557 outcomes analyzed across all academic programs, 27% were leadership related.

## Leadership Is Everyone's Responsibility

There are nearly 1,000 leadership studies and leadership development programs across college campuses in the United States (Brungardt, Greenleaf, Brungardt, & Arensdorf, 2006). Curricular leadership studies programs can be found within a variety of academic disciplines (Brungardt et al., 2006) such as sociology, business, psychology, humanities, liberal arts, professional studies, education, and agriculture. Co-curricular leadership development programs are often offered through student affairs units and are available to students regardless of major. However, other than placing leadership studies programs in a variety of academic disciplines and offering leadership development programs for students of any major, it has been difficult to quantifiably measure to what extent leadership education is cross-disciplinary and embedded throughout the institution. Developing students as leaders is not relegated to those in one academic discipline or one degree level or in academic affairs or student affairs units. Everyone in higher education must take responsibility for preparing future graduates as leaders, and doing so can offer a multitude of benefits.

**College Mission.**    The notion of developing students as leaders is embedded in many college mission statements, and this reflects the importance of graduating future leaders who can positively contribute to society (Troyer, 2004). As discussed in Chapter 1, integrating the concept of leadership within college mission statements is more than just fancy jargon for use by public relations; it is a call to action for the institution to offer opportunities to develop the leadership competencies of its students so college graduates are prepared to tackle community problems and engage in leadership to solve complex issues (Baum, Ma, & Payea, 2013). This can support the notion that subsidizing public higher education with taxpayer money is critical because there is a societal benefit to graduating leaders who can positively impact their communities.

**Accreditation.**    The notion that leadership is embedded into the learning outcomes required for accreditation across academic programs and degree levels is a message that rings loud and clear. Leadership competency development is important for all students, regardless of major or intended career field. Since the accreditation and reaccreditation processes involve articulating how each learning outcome is being met, it is critical that academic units demonstrate student learning of leadership competencies embedded in their academic programs. But, it is more than just saying that leadership development is happening; the curriculum must include leadership. And given the widespread prevalence of leadership competencies across majors, leadership development is or should be happening in nearly every academic program.

**Career Preparation.**    Since the top five skills sought by prospective employers are leadership skills and not technical skills (National Association of Colleges and Employers, 2013), a focus on leadership competency development provides students what they need to be successful in their career fields. Employers want emerging leaders who can lead when they are hired and who can then possibly grow with the organization into formal leadership roles, thus deepening the organization's talent pool. In addition, having employees with leadership competencies at all levels can contribute to productive team membership, quality decision making, and even innovation. To meet the needs of today's employers, higher education must be able to graduate students who have technical competence and proficiency in leadership.

**Common Language.**    Leadership competencies can be used across curricular and co-curricular programs (Bolden & Gosling, 2006; Conger & Ready, 2004; Seemiller & Murray, 2013) and can be built into the culture of the institution so that faculty, staff, administrators, and students interact with a common language of competencies throughout their experiences at the institution. Students may take a competency assessment at orientation, see competency language in institutional and programmatic marketing, and integrate competency language in their resumes and portfolios through interacting with career advisors. Academic advisors can help each student select a major and classes based on the competencies the student needs to develop. Faculty and staff can offer curriculum individually and jointly that explicitly integrates competencies; standard measurements can be utilized across the institution to measure competency development; and similar courses and programs can be benchmarked using competencies to uncover effective structures and pedagogies of learning and development. Reinforcing a universal set of leadership competencies in multiple institutional contexts may help students become more comfortable in understanding what the competencies mean and enable them to effectively communicate how their competencies set them apart from other college students and graduates.

**Behavioral Benchmarking.**    Using leadership competencies in higher education provides an intentional and measurable way of developing students as leaders and can create a mechanism for behavioral benchmarking (McDaniel, 2002). Faculty, staff, and administrators can create student leadership development goals appropriate for each course, volunteer/employment role, and program/event and integrate a standard set of measurements to learn the contexts in which students might develop particular competencies most effectively. This would assist in refining the curriculum and experiences to maximize leadership competency development, and it would shed light on institutional best practices. For information on evaluation measurements, including setting up an evaluation protocol and a link to free online evaluation measurements, see *The Student Leadership Competencies Guidebook* (Seemiller, 2013).

## Institutionalizing a Leadership Competency-Based Approach

Where does an institution begin in attempting to utilize a leadership competency-based approach? The following eight guidelines can help with this process.

1. Put together a task force of faculty, staff, administrators, and students to determine which leadership competencies will be used in the

institution. The task force should include individuals who can both communicate and advocate for the use of competencies and others who have involvement in a course, program, or role that would heavily incorporate leadership competencies; essentially, the task force would be the stakeholders of the integration of leadership competencies across the institution. This task force should identify the select list of competencies that will become the institution's core competencies and then encourage individual units, departments, and programs to enhance that list with additional competencies from the master list of student leadership competencies (Seemiller, 2013). Selection of the core competencies can be based on institutional values/mission, models/theories/frameworks, or institutional preference. In addition, the task force should determine the courses and/or programs into which the competencies will be integrated.

2.  Once the task force has determined which competencies will be used and where they will be used, those who will be asked to incorporate competencies into their curricula or co-curricula must be brought into the process. In order for this to be successful, those being asked to use competencies must understand the competencies, their value, and how to use them effectively. It may be best to first identify competency champions who would be willing to pilot the integration and measurement of competencies into their courses and/or programs. This can be helpful so there is a more contained pilot group with which to evaluate the effectiveness of the competencies themselves, the process of integration, and the measurements before launching the process institutionally. In addition, finding competency champions allows individuals who develop knowledge on using competencies after having been a part of the pilot serve as competency ambassadors to help bring on board other faculty, staff, and administrators (both philosophically and technically). True competency integration needs to be something in which there is buy-in from the users. If not, faculty, staff, and administrators may just go through the motions of integrating competencies, and students may not take the time to self-evaluate correctly; both situations can undermine the purpose and effectiveness of institution-wide competency use.

3.  The next step is to map the competencies across all courses and/or programs to get a bigger picture of the competency development across campus that already exists. List each course or program being measured and indicate which core competencies and student leadership competencies (Seemiller, 2013) are integrated. Are there too many courses and/or programs focusing on one competency, or perhaps not enough focusing on a core competency? This process can provide the impetus to add or modify courses or programs to focus on core competencies deemed to be critical by the institution.

4. Using the competency map to determine the prevalence of competencies across programs and courses, especially the institution's core competencies, can highlight any competency gaps. Thus, existing courses and/or programs may need to be modified and/or new ones may need to be created to fill those gaps.

5. Once competencies have been identified and embedded into the curriculum and co-curriculum, it is important to determine how to measure students' learning and development. It will be critical to discern whether the institution will be using established evaluation tools, such as those associated with *The Student Leadership Competencies Guidebook* (Seemiller, 2013); developing institution-specific measurements; or using another predetermined assessment. When those measurements are determined, the task force must consider the method of data collection. How frequently will data be collected? How will it be collected (paper or online)? Where will the data be stored? Who will analyze it? Will there be benchmarking between courses and/or programs and/or roles?

6. Competencies can also be used in marketing. If all units are using a common language around leadership competencies, students will hear and experience it over and over again. This will give legitimacy to the campus-wide effort as well as help students internalize this common language. Having one set of competencies reinforced in all elements of their collegiate experience can help students easily reflect on and communicate their leadership competencies through their resumes, portfolios, leadership and involvement transcripts, graduate school applications, and scholarship applications and during their job interviews. In addition, by having a common language of leadership competencies associated with each course and/or program, students can make more informed choices about participating in experiences that develop the competencies they need (individually determined or determined by their academic program). One way to enact this common language may be by developing icons for each of the competencies and including them in syllabi, program marketing, and other institutional documents so that students have a visual aid that draws them into competencies and communicates which competencies a course or program might focus on. If an institution is considering integrating a badging program, developing badges around specific experiences that include particular preset competencies might provide a useful and universal way to do that. For instance, a badge in civic engagement might involve predetermined experiences that include competencies such as social justice, advocating for a point of view, ethics, social responsibility, service, and creating change.

7. Tying leadership competencies to positional experiences can also be useful. Whether that includes a volunteer role, such as being a

member of student government, or a role linked to academics, such as being a research assistant or a student employee, integrating intentional competency development into the role can help develop students as leaders. Competencies can also be integrated into job trainings and duties and measured in the same way as they would be for courses and programs. Not only would the institution be able to receive feedback about leadership growth and development of its students, but supervisors and advisors could also use the data to provide goals and opportunities for each student to develop critical competencies.

8. Finally, data collected on competency development could be used to tell the institutional story, and that story may support accreditation, funding streams, and student recruitment efforts.

## Conclusion

Leadership competency development is an essential component of higher education, whether that is due to the centrality of leadership in institutional mission statements, the desire of employers to hire graduates who have leadership competencies, or because 100% of programmatic accrediting organizations require leadership-competency development of students. Leadership-competency development cannot be left to a handful of individuals on campus; it is the responsibility of everyone in higher education to ensure college graduates are also society's leaders.

## References

American College Personnel Association/National Association of Student Personnel Administrators. (2004). *Learning reconsidered: A campus-wide focus on the student experience*. Washington, DC: Author.

Bartram, D. (2005). The great eight competencies: A criterion-centric approach to validation. *Journal of Applied Psychology, 90*(6), 1185–1203.

Baum, S., Ma, J., & Payea, K. (2013). *Education pays 2013*. Retrieved from http://trends.collegeboard.org/sites/default/files/education-pays-2013-full-report.pdf

Bolden, R., & Gosling, J. (2006). Leadership competencies: Time to change the tune? *Leadership, 2*(2), 147–163.

Boyatzis, R. E. (1982). *The competent manager: A model for effective performance*. New York, NY: Wiley.

Brungardt, C., Greenleaf, J., Brungardt, C., & Arensdorf, J. (2006). Majoring in leadership: A review of undergraduate leadership degree programs. *Journal of Leadership Education, 5*(1), 4–25.

Conger, J. A., & Ready, D. A. (2004). Rethinking leadership competencies. *Leader to Leader, 32*, 41–47.

Costin, D. E. (2009). *A leadership competency model for U.S. Air Force wing chaplains* (Defense Technical Information Center document). Retrieved from http://handle.dtic.mil/100.2/ADA540058

Council for the Advancement of Standards in Higher Education. (2008). *CAS standards.* Fort Collins, CO: Author.

Defillippi, R. J., & Arthur, M. B. (2006). The boundaryless career: A competency-based perspective. *Journal of Organizational Behavior, 15*(4), 307–324.

Eaton, J. (2011). *An overview of U.S. accreditation.* Retrieved from http://chea.org /pdf/Overview%20of%20US%20Accreditation%2003.2011.pdf

Ennis, M. R. (2008). *Competency models: A review of the literature and the role of the employment and training administration (ETA)* (pp. 1–25). Office of Policy Development and Research, Employment and Training Administration, U.S. Department of Labor. Washington, DC.

Garman, A. N., & Johnson, M. P. (2006). Leadership competencies: An introduction. *Journal of Healthcare Management, 51*(1), 13–17.

Higher Education Research Institute. (1996). *A social change model of leadership development: Guidebook version III.* College Park, MD: National Clearinghouse for Leadership Programs.

Horey, J., Fallesen, J. J., Morath, R., Cronin, B., & Cassella, R. (2004). *Competency based future leadership requirements.* Fairfax, VA: Caliber Associates.

Klein, S. (1997, November). *Competencies for the future.* Paper presented at the International Seminar, Lisbon, Portugal.

Klein-Collins, R., Ikenberry, S. O., & Kuh, G. D. (2014). Competency-based education: What the board needs to know. *Trusteeship, 1*(22), 29–33.

Komives, S. R., Lucas, N., & McMahon, T. R. (1998). *Exploring leadership: For college students who want to make a difference.* San Francisco, CA: Jossey-Bass.

Kouzes, J. M., & Posner, B. Z. (1995). *The leadership challenge: How to keep getting extraordinary things done in organizations.* San Francisco, CA: Jossey-Bass.

Lawler, E. E. (1994). From job-based to competency-based organizations. *Journal of Organizational Behavior, 15*(1), 3–15.

McClelland, D. C. (1973). Testing for "competence" rather than intelligence. *American Psychologist, 28,* 1–14.

McDaniel, E. A. (2002). Senior leadership in higher education: An outcomes approach. *Journal of Leadership & Organizational Studies, 9*(2), 80–89.

Morgeson, F. P., Campion, M. A., & Levashina, J. (2009). Why don't you just show me? Performance interviews for skill-based promotions. *International Journal of Selection and Assessment, 17*(2), 203–218.

Mulder, M., Gulikers, J., Wesselink, R., & Biemans, H. (2008, March). *The new competence concept in higher education: Error or enrichment?* Paper presented at American Educational Research Association Annual Conference, New York, NY. Retrieved from http://www.mmulder.nl/wp-content/uploads/2011/12/2008-03-31-Paper-Mulder-AER A-2008.pdf

National Association of Colleges and Employers. (2013). *The candidate skills/qualities employers want.* Retrieved from https://www.naceweb.org/s10022013/job-outlook-skills-quality.aspx

Posthuma, R. A., & Campion, M. A. (2008). Twenty best practices for just employee performance reviews: Employers can use a model to achieve performance reviews that increase employee satisfaction, reduce the likelihood of litigation, and boost motivation. *Compensation & Benefits Review, 40*(1), 47–55.

Russ-Eft, D. (1995). Defining competencies: A critique. *Human Resource Development Quarterly, 6*(4), 329–335.

Seemiller, C. (2013). *The student leadership competencies guidebook.* San Francisco, CA: Jossey-Bass.

Seemiller, C., & Murray, T. (2013). The common language of leadership. *Journal of Leadership Studies, 7*(1), 33–45.

Spady, W. G. (1977). Competency based education: A bandwagon in search of a definition. *Educational Research, 6*(9), 9–14.

Spendlove, M. (2007). Competencies for effective leadership in higher education. *The International Journal for Educational Management, 21*(5), 407–417.

Troyer, M. (2004). *The challenges of leadership: A study of an emerging field* (Unpublished doctoral dissertation). University of Kentucky, Lexington.

U.S. Department of Labor. (2014). *Competency model clearinghouse.* Retrieved from http://www.careeronestop.org/CompetencyModel/

Weston, M. J., Falter, B., Lamb, G. S., Mahon, G. M., Malloch, K., Provan, K. G., … Werbylo, L. (2008). Health care leadership academy: A statewide collaboration to enhance nursing leadership competencies. *Journal of Continuing Education in Nursing, 39*(10), 468–472.

*Corey Seemiller is an assistant professor in the Organizational Leadership Program at Wright State University.*

New Directions for Higher Education • DOI: 10.1002/he

# INDEX

National Association of Student Personnel Administrators & American College Personnel Association, 70
National Defense Education Act, 1958, 27
The National Task Force on Civic Learning and Democratic Engagement, 16
Nesbit, T., 46
Ng, J. C., 49
Nohria, N., 15
Northouse, P. G., 25, 80

Olive, T. E., 28
Online classroom, 26
Ospina, S., 45, 53
Osteen, L., 7, 8, 9, 15, 20, 22, 60, 77
Owen, J. E., 77

Pak, Y. K., 49
Parker, R., 59
Participatory action research, 37, 38
Pascarella, E. T., 18, 36, 69–71
Patton, L. D., 70–71
Patton, M. Q., 63
Paul, R.W., 59
Payea, K., 98
PBL. See Problem-based learning (PBL)
Pedagogy, 46, 62
Peer-to-peer-mentoring, 53
Pendakur, V., 45, 55
Petrides, K. V., 81
Phillips, A. T., 28
Picken, J. C., 57
Popil, I., 64
Posner, B. Z., 96
Posthuma, R. A., 94
Powley, E. H., 64
President's Leadership Program, 81, 89
Prietula, M. J., 85, 86
Problem-based learning (PBL), 35; hard scaffolding, 42; institutional support for, 41; as leadership pedagogy, 36–38; learning outside of classroom, 38–39; methods and practices, 39; opportunities across the curriculum, 39–41; outcomes, 37; responsibility of learning by students, 37; soft scaffolding, 42; as tool for deep learning, 42–43; tutor in, 42
Provan, K. G., 94
Psychosocial development, 70

Psychosocial identity development, theory of, 70–71

Quinn, C. E., 25

Race-conscious leader identity, 49–50
Racism, and students of color, 48–50. See also Critical pedagogy
Ready, D. A., 99
Reisser, L., 70–74
Renn, K. A., 70–71
Rest, J. R., 36
Reynolds, M., 64
Richardson, W. C., 17
Rieffe, C., 81
Riggio, R. E., 23, 29
Roberts, D. C., 35
Rost, J. C., 6, 22–23
Rotgans, J. I., 42
Rudd, R., 25
Rudolph, F., 22
Russ-Eft, D., 93

Salovey, P., 81
Saye, J. W., 42
Schmidt, H. G., 42
Schneider, C. G., 11
Seemiller, C., 24, 93, 94, 96, 97, 99–101, 104
Service learning, 29
Shallow learning, 42
Shankman, M. L., 79, 81–83, 91
Sheridan, K., 81, 89
Shriver, M., 18
Simonetti, J. L., 64
Singleton, R. A., Jr., 12
Social change model of leadership development, 70; critical pedagogy and, 50–53; leadership, definition of, 70
Socially responsible leadership: academic autonomy and, 73–75; collaboration, importance of, 76–77; deepening of, through academic pursuits, 70–75; development of, 69–77; educational involvement, 71–73; mission-centered and mission-driven work, role of, 76; and social change model of leadership development, 70; students' capacities for, increasing of, 75–76; studies of, 70; total capacity for, 74

# NEW DIRECTIONS FOR HIGHER EDUCATION
## ORDER FORM SUBSCRIPTION AND SINGLE ISSUES

### DISCOUNTED BACK ISSUES:

Use this form to receive 20% off all back issues of *New Directions for Higher Education*.
All single issues priced at **$23.20** (normally $29.00)

TITLE                                    ISSUE NO.          ISBN

_____    _____    _____

_____    _____    _____

_____    _____    _____

*Call 1-800-835-6770 or see mailing instructions below. When calling, mention the promotional code JBNND to receive your discount. For a complete list of issues, please visit www.josseybass.com/go/ndhe*

### SUBSCRIPTIONS: (1 YEAR, 4 ISSUES)

☐ New Order          ☐ Renewal

     U.S.                 ☐ Individual: $89     ☐ Institutional: $335
     CANADA/MEXICO   ☐ Individual: $89     ☐ Institutional: $375
     ALL OTHERS       ☐ Individual: $113    ☐ Institutional: $409

*Call 1-800-835-6770 or see mailing and pricing instructions below.*
*Online subscriptions are available at www.onlinelibrary.wiley.com*

### ORDER TOTALS:

Issue / Subscription Amount: $ _____

Shipping Amount: $ _____
*(for single issues only – subscription prices include shipping)*

**Total Amount:** $ _____

| SHIPPING CHARGES: | |
| --- | --- |
| First Item | $6.00 |
| Each Add'l Item | $2.00 |

*(No sales tax for U.S. subscriptions. Canadian residents, add GST for subscription orders. Individual rate subscriptions must be paid by personal check or credit card. Individual rate subscriptions may not be resold as library copies.)*

### BILLING & SHIPPING INFORMATION:

☐ **PAYMENT ENCLOSED:** *(U.S. check or money order only. All payments must be in U.S. dollars.)*

☐ **CREDIT CARD:** ☐ VISA ☐ MC ☐ AMEX

    Card number _____ Exp. Date _____

    Card Holder Name_____ Card Issue # _____

    Signature _____ Day Phone_____

☐ **BILL ME:** *(U.S. institutional orders only. Purchase order required.)*

    Purchase order # _____
               Federal Tax ID 13559302 • GST 89102-8052

Name_____

Address_____

Phone_____ E-mail_____

Copy or detach page and send to:   **John Wiley & Sons, One Montgomery Street, Suite 1000, San Francisco, CA 94104-4594**

Order Form can also be faxed to:   **888-481-2665**

PROMO JBNND